IN A QUIET
SORT OF WAY

Roger Mott

Pen Press Publishers Ltd

First published in Great Britain by
Pen Press Publishers Ltd
The Old School
39 Chesham Road
Brighton BN2 1NB

ISBN 1-905203-77-2

Printed and bound in the UK

A catalogue record of this book is available from
the British Library

Cover design by Jacqueline Abromeit

ABOUT THE AUTHOR

Dr Roger Mott is an historian and has previously written articles on Richard II, the subject of his thesis. He has always been interested in family history, but this is the first time that he has written a biography. He was Deputy Headmaster of King's College, Taunton until his retirement in 2003. He is married  with three sons and three grandchildren and lives in Somerset.

CONTENTS

PREFACE

This is the story of Charles Mott, my great grandfather, and the parallel lives of his two eldest sons – Roger and Geoffrey. Charles is brought to life by his diaries for 1878 to 1884 - with some dates missing – which are written in a vivid and revealing style and tell much of him, his family and his interests.

Roger wrote his reminiscences later in his life and they, together with some of his letters, are written in a beautiful style which enables him to paint a very vivid picture of his world and his life. Geoffrey was also a great diary keeper and in his later years he produced his memoirs. These are written in a chronological approach and provide a mass of detail, without as many personal comments.

By using these and other sources of information I have tried to capture the essence of their lives, putting them together as thematically and episodically as possible, rather than simply in diary form. I have also tried to combine what Roger and Geoffrey were doing at different periods of their lives as their paths crossed so much and they followed similar yet different directions. Their brother Louis, for whom I have only an outline of his life, only features intermittently in the book, but I remember especially his twinkling eyes and sense of humour.

I am also fortunate to have known both Roger, my grandfather, and uncle Geoff – the latter for longer as he lived to such a great age. They all live in my memory and I hope that they would approve of what I have written.

KEY CONNECTIONS

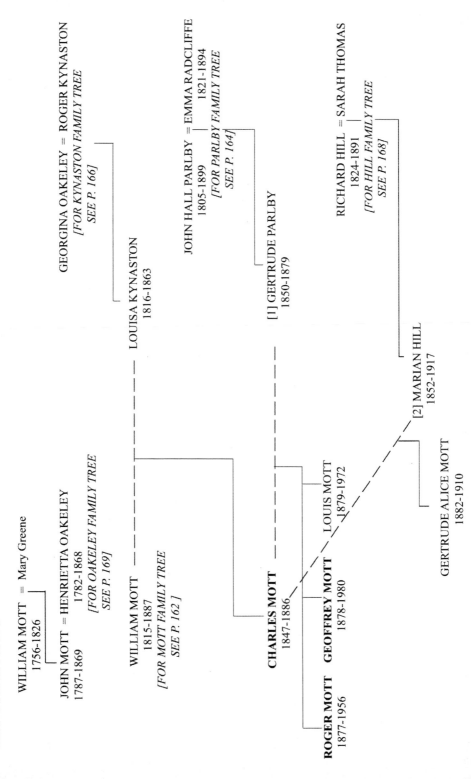

WILLIAM MOTT = Mary Greene
1756-1826

JOHN MOTT = HENRIETTA OAKELEY
1787-1869   1782-1868
              [FOR OAKELEY FAMILY TREE
              SEE P. 169]

GEORGINA OAKELEY = ROGER KYNASTON
[FOR KYNASTON FAMILY TREE
SEE P. 166]

WILLIAM MOTT
1815-1887
[FOR MOTT FAMILY TREE
SEE P. 162]

LOUISA KYNASTON
1816-1863

JOHN HALL PARLBY = EMMA RADCLIFFE
1805-1899   1821-1894
[FOR PARLBY FAMILY TREE
SEE P. 164]

[1] GERTRUDE PARLBY
1850-1879

RICHARD HILL = SARAH THOMAS
1824-1891
[FOR HILL FAMILY TREE
SEE P. 168]

CHARLES MOTT
1847-1886

LOUIS MOTT
1879-1972

[2] MARIAN HILL
1852-1917

ROGER MOTT   GEOFFREY MOTT
1877-1956   1878-1980

GERTRUDE ALICE MOTT
1882-1910

INTRODUCTION

On 6 April 1879 Gertrude Constance Mott died at the tragically young age of 28, an event described by her husband, Charles, as "the end of all my earthly hopes". 'Birdie', as Charles affectionately called her, had been taken seriously ill on their return voyage from India and had to be taken off the ship at Malta. Charles' diary records how, at 6.30 a.m. that April day, his wife's nurse, Carmela, called him to come immediately.

"I found my own darling evidently sinking fast. I had so hoped that when she began apparently to get better a few days ago, she would have gone on and I might have been allowed to take her to England, but God willed otherwise. I remained with her to the last. She spoke kindly to me, and took my hand in hers where it remained 'til her spirit had fled. I am utterly brokenhearted. Our love for one another surpassed all earthly love - I only fear it was too great."

The following day, Charles selected a burial plot for her, where "we laid the mortal remains of my darling treasure in their last resting place in the beautiful little Braxia Cemetery. Such a sweet spot. Oh, if it were only in England, but God be praised I have earnest hope that my darling herself is in heaven where I pray God I may join her". The inscription reads: "To the memory of Gertrude, the dearly loved wife of Lieut. C. A. Mott."

Charles and Gertrude had been married for only two years and nine months, and her death left him with their three small children to look after: Roger John Kynaston, who was born in Aldershot on 20 March 1877; Geoffrey Radcliffe, who was born in Bareilly, India on 23 March 1878; and Louis Oakeley, who was born in Malta on 16 March 1879. Charles wrote: "May I be enabled to bring them up as their darling Mother would have done, by God's help."

Charles Augustus Mott, the subject of the first part of this book, was born at a manor house called Wall, near Lichfield in Staffordshire in 1847, the sixth of ten children of William and Louisa Mott. Wall came into the possession of the Mott family through Charles' great-grandfather, another William Mott (1756-1826), whose life and achievements are worth recounting briefly here, as they were to prove enormously beneficial for future generations of Motts, including Charles.

William must have been a remarkable man. He was the youngest child of John and Sarah Mott, and he moved from the family's roots at Penn in Staffordshire, where they had lived since at least the late 17th century, to Lichfield, where he became very successful.[1] He was articled as a clerk at the age of 18; he then became a lawyer and a proctor in the Bishop's Consistory Court and acquired two offices – deputy diocesan registrar of the Diocese of Lichfield in 1781, and registrar to the dean and chapter in 1799 – which he retained until his death in 1826. With the principal diocesan registrar absent for most of the time and deputing everything to William, with the promise that he would "ratify and confirm" all of his actions, it is clear that, as Charles' eldest son Roger (the subject of the second part of this book) wrote later, "these two offices brought him in a good deal of money".

William's portrait shows him as a substantial and serious-minded man with 'a strong face'. His impressive achievements are well chronicled in his will, which runs to no less than 18 pages. This document details the substantial amount of property he acquired during his lifetime - including "my newly-erected Capital Mansion House, situated in the close of the cathedral Church of Lichfield"[2]; a half part of the Manor of Wall in Staffordshire, with 43 acres; a fourth part of the Manor of Tettenhall in Staffordshire; the Manor of Meysey Hampton in Gloucestershire, with approximately 690 acres (otherwise known as Maisey Hampton); lands at Kingston Bagpuize in Berkshire; and numerous other acquisitions in Staffordshire and elsewhere - as well as his various investments in government stocks, public funds, canals and other public companies, and numerous rents and tithes arising from his properties.

---

[1] See Key Connections, p. vi and Mott Family Tree, p. 162
[2] William's will shows the extent of his Capital Mansion House, with its "Coach House, Granary, Brewhouse, Stables, Outbuildings and Gardens or Pleasure Ground belonging to it all of which are freehold of inheritance".

With all these acquisitions amounting to over 1,000 acres, William had raised his family into the landed interest and he is referred to in deeds as 'a gentleman'. It is clear from his will that he made very careful and detailed provision for his son and two daughters[3], and also tried to provide for his grandchildren. Indeed, despite some rather profligate behaviour at times, four future generations of Motts were able to benefit from his success.

As a gentleman, William was able to give his son (and Charles' grandfather) John tenements and lands amounting to 160 acres, as a prenuptial marriage settlement to enable him to marry Henrietta Oakeley, 'a beautiful woman' and the eldest daughter of Sir Charles Oakeley, who had rented the Bishop's Palace in the Close at Lichfield, near to where the Motts lived, in 1810, after retiring from the post of Governor of Madras.[4] At the time of William's death, John was left in trust a considerable amount of property, including his new Capital Mansion House at Lichfield; Wall House; a quarter share of the manor of Tettenhall; the manor of Meysey Hampton; and many other properties which his father had purchased.

Unfortunately, as Roger points out, John (1787-1869) did not inherit his father's financial acumen and "spent a lot of the family money". He was well set-up by his father as a proctor in the Bishop's Consistory Court and deputy registrar, and was described by Charles' brother Edward as "a proctor in a big way of business"[5], but his temperament and interests led him in other directions. He commanded the Lichfield Troop of the Staffordshire Yeomanry and was very fond of horses and racing which Roger comments, "seems somewhat odd for a proctor and registrar of a cathedral!" Indeed his grandson, Edward, was told how he "used to go racing on the sly when he ought to have been drawing up ladies' and gentlemen's wills".[6] He was also clearly an outgoing person, and took Edward

---

[3] William was able to leave his property at Kingston Bagpuize, Berkshire, to his daughter Sarah, who had married Adam Blandy. His other daughter, Maria Greene, who had married Reverend Thomas Fell, Rector of Sheepy and Prebendary of Lichfield, was also well provided for, and the two daughters were left the bulk of their father's plate, besides their settlement money.

[4] See Key Connections, p. vi and Oakeley Family Tree, p. 169

[5] E.S. Mott, *A Mingled Yarn* (London, 1898), p. 3. Edward Mott's autobiography contains very little information about his family, but he does make occasional comments which provide an invaluable insight from his own perspective. In particular, he brings his father and grandfather to life in a way that no other source of information is able to do.

[6] *A Mingled Yarn* p. 31

to meet racing celebrities when Edward's less extrovert father was not inclined to attend. John was able to live 'in good style', as shown by the portraits of him and his wife, in which he is wearing his yeomanry uniform and she an impressive ermine cloak.

The result of all this was that, as Roger put it, the pace of his spending was "too hot, for on his death the house in the close and its contents were sold". So, William's Mansion House went out of the family's control and Charles commented in his diary for 1883 that he "had tea with the Moberlys, in the old house in the close which I had not been in since my grandfather's death now 14 years ago". By the time of his death, John had also sold other property in Staffordshire, as well as the Tettenhall estate, so the property left to his son William consisted of Wall, some other lands in Staffordshire and the manor of Meysey Hampton.

However, despite these property sales, Charles' father William (1815-1887) was also able to live in some style and to spend his legacy too liberally as he was "rather too fond of racing and died poor". William married his first cousin, Louisa Ann Kynaston – 'their mothers being sisters'. (This happened because one of Sir Charles Oakeley's daughters, Henrietta, had married John Mott, and another, Georgina, had married Roger Kynaston.[7]) William and Louisa married at St George's Church in London's Hanover Square in 1837.

William was educated at Eton and Christ Church, Oxford, from where he graduated in 1836. After Oxford, he went on 'the grand tour' before settling down at Wall, where, in keeping with his position in society, he performed valuable functions as Deputy Lord Lieutenant of Staffordshire and as a Justice of the Peace. In his capacity as Deputy Lord Lieutenant, according to his son Edward, he was entitled "to appear before his sovereign on state occasions in a handsome uniform". As a JP, he appeared in less glamorous settings, and Edward remembers that he "periodically dispensed justice on the first-floor of an alehouse at Muckely Corner, a village on the edge of the Black Country, and the sound equity of the decisions of 'Mott o' Wall', when dealing with a pugnacious collier or night-poacher of murderous intent, was never questioned".[8]   He

---

[7] See Key Connections, p. vi and Oakeley Family Tree, p. 169
[8] *A Mingled Yarn,* p. 2

also commanded the Lichfield Troop of the Staffordshire Yeomanry for many years and there is a portrait of him in uniform as a young man. Roger remembered his grandfather well when he was older and says that "he was a fine, good-looking man".

William was described by his son Edward as being "of a retiring habit" and "particular as to his acquaintances" – someone very much at home with his friends, but "rather shy" of large-scale entertaining.[9] His wife Louisa "was an excellent musician and a very charming person", and they had ten children together before she died at the age of 46 in 1863. William remarried in 1867, his new wife being a widow by the name of Anna Maria Ward, who was described by Edward as "a clever woman of the world, with a charm of manner that at once endeared her to myself".[10] The couple moved from Wall, which was let out, to St Leonards, on the south coast, where they lived during the 1880s.

By the time of Charles' marriage to Gertrude in 1876, only three of his nine brothers or sisters were still alive and he was the youngest. Five of his siblings had died in infancy by 1857 ("it looks as if the nursery at Wall was not a very healthy place or else the children were delicate, possibly as the result of their parents being first cousins") and another of his sisters, Henrietta - "the beauty of the family with lovely long hair" - had died two years before Charles got married.

Charles' eldest surviving brother was Reverend William Kynaston Mott, who was known as Willie. He followed in his father's footsteps to Eton and Christ Church, Oxford, and was a good cricketer, being one of the original Free Foresters. He remained unmarried and took holy orders, becoming curate of Heavitree, near Exeter, where he was living in lodgings at the time of the census of 1881. He also spent time at the Oxford and Cambridge Club in London and often met Charles there when they were both in the city. William, who was the heir to the family estates, was always very reliable and generous, using what Edward describes as his "gentle logic"[11] to provide invaluable help to his two brothers on more than one occasion, including when he helped Charles to get married. His sister Louise, known as Sissie, lived in St Austell in Cornwall with her

---

[9] *A Mingled Yarn*, p. 274
[10] *A Mingled Yarn*, p. 242
[11] *A Mingled Yarn*, p. 249

husband, Arthur Coode, a banker, and they were also to prove a great support to Charles.

However, Charles' other brother, Edward, who wrote *A Mingled Yarn* in which he painted himself as 'the bad boy of the family', had a very chequered career. He started out in the army, in the 19th First Yorks Regiment of Foot, serving on the frontiers of India, but, when purchasing the rank of lieutenant necessitated a transfer to Burma, he went absent without leave for seven months, was confined for desertion and advised to send in an application to retire by selling his commission. But fortune came to his rescue: he was released from confinement and told not to sell his commission, but to return home and then go back to India in a year or so. To do this he had to pay off his debts, which he did with his winnings from a horse race meeting, and to get himself sent back to England for medical reasons, which he also managed. His father had always been, in Edward's own words, "an over-indulgent parent"[12] and on his return to England he "came up to town … to welcome the prodigal as soon as possible. He neither uttered, nor looked, one word of reproach … but there was that in his face which betrayed the belief that I was booked for another world."[13] He did indeed move into "another world" – he "'loafed' a great deal"[14] before deciding he could not face returning to India and left the army, "much to the wrath and disgust of my father."[15] As a confirmed gambler, having spent his allowance in advance and borrowed money, "native obstinacy" stopped him using the family home, which was "still open to me", and he ended up "sleeping in the open" on the Embankment and in St James' Park until his elder brother, William, "eventually ran me down"[16] and persuaded him to be rescued. He subsequently tried his hand as a strolling actor, before becoming a journalist for the 'Pink Un' (The Sporting Times) under the name of Nathaniel Gubbins.

Charles himself was born on 16 November 1847 and he followed his two elder brothers to Drummer, a preparatory school for Eton that was known, according to Edward, "to many aristocratic parents as 'The Little House of Lords'"[17], before going on to Eton and Sand-

---

[12] *A Mingled Yarn*, p. 63
[13] *A Mingled Yarn*, p. 240
[14] *A Mingled Yarn*, p. 241
[15] *A Mingled Yarn*, p. 243
[16] *A Mingled Yarn*, p. 249
[17] *A Mingled Yarn*, p. 5

hurst. He must have had to live down Edward's reputation at both establishments, but, unlike his brother, he followed the lifestyle that was expected of him and was gazetted to the Second Queen's Royal Regiment of Foot, joining them in Bermuda as an ensign in 1865.

PART ONE
CHARLES MOTT

CHAPTER ONE

CHARLES AND GERTRUDE

Charles' early postings as an ensign in the Queen's Royal Regiment included Bermuda and Galway in Ireland. However, in 1871 he was promoted to lieutenant and stationed at Raglan Barracks in Devonport, and it was here that he first met Gertrude Constance Parlby. Charles' son Roger relates how "the Parlbys' were hospitable folk, and Plymouth, being both a naval and a military station, officers of both services always had a welcome at (their house) Manadon. In the 1870s there were four grown-up daughters, and the favourite of the young men was Gertrude Constance. Among her admirers was Lieutenant Charles Augustus Mott of the Queen's Royal Regiment, and the two fell deeply in love with each other."

According to Roger, his father was "very good-looking" and "very popular with everybody", while his mother, Gertrude, "must have been an attractive girl, petite, brown hair and eyes full of fun, and at the same time deeply religious. She used to share a bedroom with her favourite sister, Mildred, at the top of the house, and I remember her sister telling me that Gertrude used occasionally to walk in her sleep, and that she once saw her get up, wash her face and hands and return to bed without waking."

Gertrude's father, Reverend John Hall Parlby, was the owner of a considerable estate, Manadon, and a 'squarson' – a squire and a parson - although he did not exercise clerical duties himself.[18] He "considered that Charles (as a younger son) could not afford to keep a wife" and he refused to sanction an engagement with his daughter. Roger relates how "at that time, the Manadon letters were all delivered at the house in a locked leather bag of which Mr Parlby kept the key, so correspondence between the young lovers was impossible through the ordinary channel. But Gertrude had a clever

---

[18] See Key Connections p. vi and Parlby Family Tree p.164

fox terrier, Puck, and she trained him to take her letters to the lodge (half a mile from the house) for transmission by the lodge-keeper to the postman and Puck would bring Charlie's letters back to his mistress!"

However, despite all this secret correspondence there seemed little prospect of them getting married. We know that Charles' father had been unable to afford to send his elder son Edward into a cavalry regiment, as he "had qualms on the subject of the necessary expenditure";[19] and Charles would not have had a sufficient allowance to enable him to marry. It was through the generosity of his eldest brother, William, that Charles was able to persuade his prospective father-in-law that he could now provide a marriage settlement.

Charles was also helped by the fact that, in 1869, his father had left him and his brother Edward 57 acres of land at Sedgley in Staffordshire, which had been purchased by their great-grandfather William, and these acres were sold in July 1876 for £1,300. Charles' share must have helped his position considerably and the wedding went ahead in Pennycross church, close to Manadon, on 20 June 1876.

Charles' regimental duties soon took the newly-married couple to Aldershot, where their eldest son Roger was to be born on 20 March 1877. However, three months later the battalion was ordered to India and Charles had to set sail with Gertrude and Roger. When they arrived in Malta, *en route*, there was a war scare and the cabin, which Roger and his nurse were occupying, had to be surrendered for the use of a senior officer. Roger had to be sent back to England in the care of his nurse, and another lady who was returning home and, on arrival he went to Manadon, where he was accommodated in Gertrude's mother's bedroom. Having to send their child home in this way must have been a worrying ordeal for his parents and Charles' diary records that on 30 March 1878 "heard of safe arrival of darling Roger at Manadon. Thank God!" Roger, nevertheless, settled in well. "I was the first of her grandchildren and was probably made much of in consequence." Manadon was to be his home for the next two years.

At Bareilly in India on Saturday 23 March 1878, Charles writes:

---

[19] *A Mingled Yarn* p. 68

4

"my darling wife Birdie was safely delivered of a (second) son (Geoffrey) at 9 a.m. She was only taken ill at five. Up to the present, both mother and child are doing as well as possible." And the following day he adds "my darling wife continues wonderfully well and the infant likewise. Sat with Birdie nearly all day."

He soon felt justified in telegraphing to Manadon that they were both progressing well and "Birdie was moved from one bed to another and she seems very cheerful". He was able to write on 29 March "it is such a blessing that all is going on well at our house. The doctor thinks his task is about over." Three days later "my darling wife" was "getting on beautifully" and "she sat in the drawing room for some time". "The infant was christened Geoffrey Radcliffe Mott on 17 April at 7.45 a.m." and three days later they heard from Gertrude's mother and sister Mildred that they had received the telegrams telling of his birth.

However, the heat of the plains was considerable and Birdie was "suffering a good deal at times from neuralgia". By June the weather was "getting fearfully hot, and the hot winds are dreadful". Charles "had to go the funerals of two poor fellows - the second double funeral we have had during the last few days." Therefore he applied to go to the hills to Naini Tal to enable his wife and son to escape the heat of the plains. When they were packing up he won the regimental sweepstake on the Derby "amounting to 123 rupees. A very nice little help to us, as we are very hard up, with these constant moves." But with very hot weather and "the winds something frightful" they were glad to be on the move. However, "everything seemed to go wrong" on the journey and by the time they had ascended the hill to Naini Tal from Ranibagh they were all exhausted and "my darling wife was very unwell".

The trip to the hills "did not produce any good effect" on Gertrude and he was concerned that "my darling wife was very unwell indeed, and I am most anxious and uncomfortable about her". But while "she does not improve in the least, baby (Geoffrey) looks the very picture of health". He turned down an invitation to go for a ride because he "didn't like to leave my darling wife who continues far from well".

Nevertheless things did improve. Their heavy luggage arrived and the house they had chosen began to look a little more homely. On their wedding anniversary, Charles was "hard at work all the morning decorating the drawing room. It soon began to look nice."

He wrote: "thank God for sparing us to one another for so long. May my darling soon recover." And by the end of the month she "really seems a little better. Please God she may continue to improve."

During July and August Gertrude was able to go out with him - for example on 22 August, having gone home in the rain from the depot, they were then able to go to dinner at Government House. Charles was also able to pursue one of his great interests, the theatre, and he got involved in the production of *Ours*. The production led to an altercation over a gratuity for the bandmaster, Mr Kearns, who, feeling it was too small, became "somewhat insolent" and refused it. Arthur Barrow, who organized the theatricals, decided to give him an extra £25 but, before he could do so, Kearns wrote him a "most impertinent letter". The following day Kearns "apologized humbly for his conduct" and the matter was dropped. When *Ours* was put on, the first night was "not such a success as we should have liked, but the audience nevertheless considered it the best thing yet done here." On the next night the first and second acts went very well.

Charles, concerned about his wife, wanted to return to England and at the beginning of September he had had some good news when "a telegram arrived from Manadon to say that I had been offered the appointment of *Aide-de-Camp* (ADC) to General Sir Pollexfen Radcliffe", who was a first cousin of Gertrude's mother, Emma Parlby (*née* Radcliffe).

Charles was "very pleased and of course my darling was particularly so". She was by now three months pregnant again and not feeling well. Her mother's influence must have been a key factor in enabling Charles to get this appointment; she was clearly worried about the news she was hearing of her daughter's ill-health and anxious to have her back in England.

On 1 October Charles heard that he might possibly be sent back to England as early as the following month. "Please God it may be so". Two days later they went to a fancy dress ball with Birdie as an 18th century *Citoyenne de Paris* and Charles as a Turkish Zouave. They were also cheered to hear from Manadon and to receive a photograph of their eldest son, Roger. At the end of the month Birdie was "better in the morning but bad again at night", but by the beginning of November things seemed to be improving. They were packing up and Birdie "seems pretty well".

Returning to Bareilly however was no simple matter. Charles

began to move their things on 7 November. He "started the baggage down the hill with coolies" and then, after doing more packing, set off after lunch after saying goodbye to Birdie. He reached Ranibagh and then set off on elephants at 9.30 p.m. on a beautiful moonlit night. By 3 a.m. he had reached Nugla, but had to wait an hour for the pack elephants. By 9 a.m. they had arrived at Baherai; "no cooks or tents had come, but they were not long after us - I stayed at the Dak Bungalow, a wretched place where I could get nothing I wanted. Started again at about 8 p.m. on elephants for the next stage." Having reached their next destination, the final stage to Bareilly was in bullock carts, with the baggage on two elephants, where they arrived at 7 a.m.

During their absence he wrote to Birdie every day, receiving a letter from her on 11 November in which she enclosed a letter from her parents who were "much annoyed and very naturally, at the idiotic behaviour of Arbuthnott (Charles Arbuthnott had married Birdie's younger sister Marion) in volunteering for India after he had just paid £100 to escape coming here." Having arranged for one daughter to return from India, another was about to go in the opposite direction.

By the time they were reunited, Birdie had developed a cough "which is very troublesome at night, but otherwise she is ever so much better than she was at Naini Tal and has a splendid appetite." Birdie was also cheered by the news that the Arbuthnotts were "coming out here". The two of them were able to go out for "a little stroll", Charles bought her "a necklace and bracelets" and they heard from Manadon that "the Arbuthnotts had just left England on the *Malabar*". But Charles was "rather disturbed by seeing in the Army and Navy Gazette that Lieutenant Hutton, 60th Rifles had been appointed ADC to General Radcliffe. However I suppose it is only temporary." And when they had more news from England the letters "gave us very little satisfaction". Charles' father wrote to tell him of the death of his uncle, Herbert Kynaston, the former high master of St Paul's School, "but said not a word of his will".[20]

However, with Birdie in better health Charles was able to go out with the regimental hounds on a few occasions. They caught a jackal on one hunt and a wild cat on another. He also played in a few cricket matches, although he was hampered by a "nasty fall when

---

[20] See Kynaston Family Tree p. 166

7

fielding" which led to his knee being "very swollen and painful".

By the end of December they were busy packing up to leave India, but there were still snags. "I telegraphed to Simla to know if my leave had been signed, as I have heard nothing of it yet. Had no answer however." Finally they were able to leave Bareilly by the 4.20 p.m. train on 30 December and the following night they dined and "played games till 12 o'clock when we drank the New Year in, in Scotch whiskey to the strains of 'Auld Lang Syne'."

Charles summed up the year 1878 as a "most anxious one to me". But "thank God the end of the year sees her in very good health. Our prospects of a speedy return home are good, though we are still uncertain."

On New Year's Day 1879, Charles, ill with bronchitis, received a telegram saying that his leave was "not sanctioned". He felt unwell for the rest of that week and had a number of visits from the doctor, while he continued to worry that his leave had been refused. He "wrote back and sent in a long official statement requesting my case to be reconsidered." He also heard that his uncle, Herbert Kynaston, had left everything to Emma, his wife's maid who had a great influence over him, "but it is not supposed to be very much".

However, following his appeal, Charles' leave was sanctioned and at the beginning of February they were in Bombay, awaiting departure, with Birdie very tired. There they met up with the Arbuthnotts and Birdie was delighted to be able to spend some time with her sister Marion. But Birdie's ill-health continued to be a cause for concern: she was "very weak and feverish" on 8 February and the next day "very unwell for most of the day and stayed in bed till late in the afternoon". She "was very unwell all the day" on Friday 14 February and "stayed in bed till the evening and then saw Dr Langley who prescribed for her". By the next day she was rather better, as was Geoffrey, who had had a bad cough, and they were able to inspect their accommodation on their ship the *Trentham Hall*, which they were pleased with. Birdie was better on Sunday and the next day the Arbuthnotts came to dinner. Charles read an advertisement in the Bombay Gazette on Tuesday that the *Trentham Hall* would leave at 5 p.m. "so sent to tell Marion and made ready". This turned out to be false information as the boat was leaving at 5 p.m. the next day, but as everything was packed they went on board that night. They were able to go on shore and shop the following day, and the Arbuthnotts came for a final visit at about 4 p.m. with the latest mail before the ship sailed promptly at 5 p.m.

The voyage proved a real trial. Three days after setting sail, Birdie was "very unwell at night", but she was able to dine on deck a few days later and the ship reached the Red Sea without further incident. But on Sunday 2 March "my poor darling was very ill all day and all last night. Fever high with much pain". The following day the doctor saw her as she was "still very unwell, especially in the evening when she had some of her old liver pains again". She was "very ill indeed" on Wednesday and Charles was "quite wretched thinking what to do for her". Having passed through Port Said in the teeth of a gale on Saturday, Charles was seasick for the next two days, while Birdie was still "very ill still from liver". The following Tuesday he sat with her all day and the next day she was "still very unwell". At midnight on 12 March, when the ship docked in Malta, Dr Schembri "recommended Birdie to come ashore".

So, the two of them landed and went to the Great Britain Hotel at 8 a.m. the following morning. They decided to "send Geoffrey on with the ship to England in the care of the Hayes". Miss Jones, a nurse, came to look after Birdie. By Saturday 15 March Birdie thought that her confinement was near. Charles wrote: "may God spare her and bring her safely through it". Late in the afternoon the following day "she became worse and I went for Dr Schembri. He was only just in time to deliver her of a son (Louis Oakeley) very quickly and satisfactorily at about 7.30 p.m."

The next day she was pretty well "though she is very weak and her liver is still bad. The baby is well." That night Charles had little or no sleep on account of the child. "I slept in Birdie's room and she was able to have a better night." She was still "dreadfully weak" but she was "a little better, thank God" by Thursday 20 March. The following day, however, she was "worse than ever. So weak and ill. Dr Schembri fears an abscess. May God bring her safely through and spare us to one another if it be His will for many years. I felt miserable beyond measure. She had a fair night by means of morphia and stimulants." She was "unaccountably much easier" the following morning but Charles was "afraid to be too sanguine". She was "not so well again" on the Sunday and "the doctor made me very miserable by telling me how dangerous her state was".

The next day Dr Zaramunt saw her with Dr Schembri. He "took a much more hopeful view of her case and made me more cheerful". But she was very weak again that afternoon and had a very restless night. "I was up more than every hour." By Tuesday 25 March "all my hopes again failed me, for my darling wife was dreadfully ill again. I hardly knew what to think".

He now telegraphed her mother, Emma Parlby, to tell her of the serious state of affairs and to ask if someone could come out to Malta. Emma decided to come herself together with one of her sons, St John, who was in the navy. On hearing this news Charles was "so glad and Birdie too. Made her better at once." Her mother then telegraphed more good news from London that Geoffrey had "arrived safely in England. Thank God." On top of that Birdie was weak but not in such pain. On Friday she "seemed better than she has been for some days" and by the following Wednesday 2 April there was "still an improvement in my darling wife's condition for which I am truly thankful".

But two days later she "took a turn for the worse, which makes me most anxious". That night Carmela the nurse was to look after Birdie but she "was so bad that I sat with her not taking my clothes off, till 4 a.m." The next day her mother arrived with St John and the seriousness of the situation was immediately apparent to her. "She was *so* shocked to see my own poor darling Gertrude. *So* unlike what she was when she last saw her." That night both her mother and Charles went up to her for a short time "but left her after she had taken her opiate".

The end came the following morning on Sunday 6 April. Her mother and her brother St John were with Charles when she died. They helped him to select a burial plot in Braxia cemetery in Valetta - "mother is so kind and St John too". He also received a letter from Mildred, who would not yet have heard of her sister's death, which "only made me sadder".

The funeral service itself was a private affair as Charles had wished. He wrote that "Mr Batemen performed the ceremony *so* nicely and spoke such comforting words to me afterwards." He "reminded me that we have the assurance that those we love remember us as we remember them." After "another dreadful night with horrible dreams, succeeded by another gloomy day", the three of them set sail on a P and O steamship. Nine days later, Gerald Parlby came to meet them in Southampton and to accompany them on the train to Manadon. Charles wrote that he was "so glad to be home again, but oh, it was a very trying meeting with all again. Such kindness from all, as I can never express nor at all adequately repay.

May God bless them all, and also the hosts of people who have written letters of sympathy." He now had to face a future with three young children but without his beloved wife.

Memories of Birdie remained strong. A brass plaque was put up in her memory in Pennycross church, close to Manadon, under the stain glass window behind the altar. Charles wrote on 28 February 1880 that he had "received new photos of my darling's grave from Malta" which were "very much better than the last". Five years after her death, in 1884, he was still writing of her in his diary: on 6 April it was "the fifth anniversary of my darling Birdie's death" and on 14 August "my darling Gertrude's birthday. She would have been 34".

CHAPTER TWO

LIFE WITHOUT GERTRUDE

When Gertrude died, Charles had written "may I be enabled to bring
them up as their darling Mother would have done, by God's help."
Charles and his sons were reunited at Manadon on his return from
Malta, and Roger recollects that "my aunt Mildred (aged 27) and
the beloved family-governess, Miss Morton, (who was in her late
50s) took charge of the three of us."

Gertrude's family played a key role in the upbringing of Roger,
Geoffrey and Louis, especially her sister, aunt Mildred, and her parents. Gertrude was the daughter of Reverend John Hall Parlby, whose
father had married the heiress of Manadon near Plymouth, which
Roger describes as "one of the loveliest houses in Devon", and which
passed into the hands of the Parlby family. John Hall Parlby was
married twice and he and his family also played an important part in
Charles' life.[21]

By his first wife he had three children – Blanche, who was unmarried, Gerald, who was in the army, and Emily, who was married
to William Hole of Parke, Bovey Tracey. After his first wife died,
John Hall Parlby married Emma Radcliffe, from Warleigh on the
banks of the Tamar, three miles from Manadon, and they had nine
children, of whom seven were still alive when Gertrude died. Mildred,
known as Millie and beloved of Charles' and Gertrude's children,
was unmarried; Marion went to India with her husband, Charles,
later Viscount Arbuthnott, where they met Charles and Gertrude; St
John came out with his mother to see Charles and Gertrude in Malta;
and Winifred was soon to be married to Colonel Hugh Thurlow. The
youngest members of the family were Reginald, who was later to
inherit Manadon, and Walter and Edward, both of whom later went

---

[21] See Parlby family tree p. 164

12

to live in Canada.

Holidays at Manadon were to make an indelible impression on all the children, but Charles had already been appointed as ADC to Emma Parlby's first cousin, General Radcliffe while in India and, three days after his return, General Radcliffe wanted him to report to him. Charles wrote to his eldest brother Willie and asked him if he would accompany him, which he agreed to do. He joined him on the train at Exeter where they "had such a nice talk and he was so kind, promising that I should not lose by all the expenses I have suffered lately." Charles went on to Colchester where he stayed with the Radcliffes at Grey Friars "who were most kind". He soon took up his new role at the headquarters in Colchester, where he took a house called Plevna Lodge. When this move took place the three boys travelled there from Manadon, with the Parlby family governess, Miss Morton, together with a nurse and a nursemaid, to look after them.

Life for the children settled into a new pattern. At the beginning of 1880 Charles "went for a little drive with Miss Morton and Roger before going to the office". All the children were ill in January but were soon "somewhat better". When Charles returned from his travels at the end of the month, he found "the dear children and Miss Morton all pretty well". In March they "took the children to be photographed, but Geoffrey wouldn't be done at any price, so Roger had to be done by himself." Later in the month, with Roger growing up, Charles took him for a little walk in the afternoon and on his third birthday he was given a tea party. A month later Miss Morton and Roger drove to the woods to pick primroses.

With arrangements made for the children, Charles was able to settle into life as ADC to General Radcliffe who commanded Eastern District. He had to go to the office each morning when the general was there, but not when he was away. He rode in on his horse Rufus not always without mishap – on Ash Wednesday he "gave me a crack over the head, while I was opening the gate"; at the beginning of March "I had a spill from Rufus when going to the office"; and two weeks later "Rufus trod on a nail going to the office and lamed himself".

Like all officers in peacetime he had plenty of time to involve himself in the local community. In particular he got involved with ambulance classes, including the ladies ambulance class which was being held at the Literary Institute by Dr Gilbourne. Charles was responsible for other classes, delivering the lecture on stretchers to a male class and two days later to the working men's class who "passed a vote of thanks". He also opened large classes for the police and fire brigade and had to make arrangements for the examination of all these classes.

As an ADC, he also accompanied the general on his official duties, for example, when the regiments in garrison had some outpost duty, he went with the general to see the dispositions. In March he went to the Queen's *Levée* with General Radcliffe "where I was presented to Her Majesty by the general". When the general was appointed to command one of the opposing forces at the Volunteers Review at Brighton on Easter Monday, he wrote to secure rooms and stabling. They went down to Brighton on Maundy Thursday spending the next day looking at the ground for the review. On Easter Saturday he went to the review ground with the general and "we rode over the ground with Prince Edward". On Easter Day he went for a walk and found a "great concourse of people assembled" and for the review itself on Easter Monday he reports that there were "crowds of people" and "plenty of powder burnt" but that it was "an impossible attack". But the march past was very good and "all connected with the day was very creditable". He was clearly performing his duties well and by the end of April he had been promoted to captain and commented that it was "at last (announced) in the Gazette".

He was able to undertake a number of trips during the year. In mid January he joined his father and his second wife at St Leonards, near Hastings, for a week, before going on to visit his father's youngest brother, Charles, his wife Elizabeth and their younger son Arthur at Rugby. From there he went to Pool House, Lichfield where he was warmly welcomed by his aunts Emily and Georgiana.[22] He walked to Wall House, Lichfield owned by his father and "did a commission for Mrs Mott" and then returned the next day with Georgiana when "we had luncheon with the Stokes' who seem very nice people". They had taken over the living at Wall and lived in the vicarage. Charles records that he had "a good talk with the aunts in the evening" on his final night in Lichfield.

At the beginning of February Charles' father, William, heard that his uncle, Reverend Frederick Oakeley, had died.[23] Canon Oakeley,

---

[22] See Mott family tree p. 162
[23] See Oakeley family tree p. 169

a fellow of Balliol College, Oxford, and described as "quiet and gentle", had joined the Church of Rome in 1845 during the time of the Oxford Movement, after publicly claiming the right to believe Roman Catholic doctrines, as a result of which he was suspended from his clerical duties. He was working in a very poor parish in Islington, living a very self-denying and ascetic life when he died in 1880. William and Reverend Herbert Kynaston, a Canon of Durham and Professor of Greek and Classical Literature at Durham University, were among those who attended the funeral when, after a Requiem Mass which lasted two hours, he was buried at Kensal Green. Herbert Kynaston records that "I wrote some high verses on the occasion which were printed in the Guardian and distributed among appreciative friends."[24]

Manadon continued to feature strongly in Charles' life. He wrote to Gertrude's sister Mildred a lot and describes her with great affection as "dear Millie". On his birthday "dear Millie gave me some grape scissors". He also met her brother, St John, in January on board a Cowes boat at Southampton. But St John's fortunes took a turn for the worse a few months later when he came up to London from Manadon for medical advice. When Charles went to see him "the surgeon had discovered that he was suffering from a large lumbar abscess, somehow connected with disease of the spine. Very sad."

The start of June saw the whole family setting off for Manadon when they "left Colchester with Miss Morton, the three children and two nurses, by the 9.20 train". "Miss Morton left us at Liverpool Street. The rest of us went down by *Flying Dutchman* from Paddington. We reached Mutley about six, where Millie met us." St John was "rather better than last week". While at Manadon Charles suffered from rheumatism, but was still able to mow the lawn tennis ground, decorate a room for a concert and do some recitations, walk into Plymouth to see his sister Sissie and her husband Arthur Coode on their way to Lichfield, and go with Millie to the archery ground where there was a Lawn Tennis Tournament. He also sat with St John. At the end of June "St John's operation was successfully performed at Manadon by Durham of Guy's (Hospital)".

In August, with friends, he took a ship up the Scheldt "anything much more uninteresting can't be imagined". He landed at Antwerp

---

[24] See Kynaston family tree p. 166

and looked round the boulevards, the cathedral and the museum of antiquities. After dinner he went to some music halls. He then decided to move to Brussels, despite having previously "telegraphed for a room and had answer that there were none. However I chanced it and got a nice room. Went to the Eden Theatre after dinner - a sort of Alhambra only far more gorgeous."

But news of St John from Manadon grew worse again. Millie wrote to him of St John's "great affliction, the loss of one of his eyes". Three days later he got a telegram to say that St John was much worse "and asking me to come. I telegraphed that I would come at once". St John had sailed out to Malta when Charles needed him and Charles now did the same for him. This involved a very rough passage from Calais to Dover, which he reached about 3.30 p.m., and then to Charing Cross at 6.30 p.m. The following day he went from Paddington to Mutley from where he drove out to Manadon and "found dear St John in a dreadful state". He sat up with him all night, with the nurse. He did the same the following night when "he had a very quiet night, but, just before I was thinking of going off duty about 6.30 a.m., he was all of a sudden seized with a dreadful spasm, and I at once called the others. For full half an hour we were holding him in bed, and I never saw such a struggle for life, and hope I never may again. However, he actually got over it, and by half past eight was quite calm again. We were rubbing his hand and face for many hours during the day, and when evening came, he was quite calm, and passed a good night."

The next day he was better but was "very much exhausted after his fearful attacks. I was with him for the greater part of the day, and began to sit with him from 10 p.m." William Hole came over from Parke, Bovey Tracey and prayed with him and Gerald Parlby who had come from Christ Church, Oxford sat up with him during the night with Charles, but had to leave the following day.

St John "was very bad in the morning and I thought it was nearly the end, but he again rallied". Charles sat up with him overnight but had to call on William Hole "for two dreadful attacks". "We again thought he couldn't survive, and twice more about noon, when the doctors were with him, did he have attacks. Of course he was dreadfully weak the rest of the day, but his rally was something marvellous."

There was "apparently a wonderful rally" the following day, but "the doctors still give no hope so I suppose it is only temporary, but I can't help hoping, though I don't like to encourage it in others." St John had fish and meat, and coffee and pudding, in addition to turtle jelly and brandy and milk. "May God spare him, if it be His will, and at all events grant him a respite from further suffering."

Two days later he "had a bad cough all the morning. The doctors declared him "worse all round". About 3 p.m. "a decided change came over him. The cough had ceased, but he became very short of breath. He knew it was near his end and gave away all his little property. His intellect was unimpaired throughout, and gradually he sank, drawing his last breath at 6.30 p.m. and so peacefully passed away one whom none could know without loving, whose life and death were an example to us all."

The next morning "I saw dear St John asleep in death, looking so peaceful". His mother bore up well. Charles walked to Pontey's nursery on the Monday morning and ordered a floral naval anchor for St John's coffin and in the afternoon he went with Mrs Parlby to Pennycross Church "to see how they were getting on with the grave". On 1 September "at 10.40 we left Manadon to follow dear St John's remains to their last resting place on earth. The tenants carried the body, three reliefs of eight". There were many people at the church and "we came back soon after 12".

It was not until early September that "Blanche, Millie and I with the children, left Mutley by train for Paddington" and thus back to Colchester. Millie stayed with her uncle, General Radcliffe, and his wife at Grey Friars, while Blanche, who was Millie's eldest stepsister,[25] stayed at Charles' house with Miss Morton. Millie was soon "very unwell" and remained "not at all well" at the end of the week. But she was able to "come up to luncheon and stayed the afternoon" by the middle of the following week, and two days later Charles "walked up the town with Millie" and then "drove Blanche and Miss Morton back in time for dinner".

Charles went for a drive with Blanche and Miss Morton on a few occasions and Blanche gave him a driving whip for his birthday. After a month Blanche went to stay with General Radcliffe and his wife at Grey Friars while Millie was "to have come to stay with me", but was still "not well enough" to move for a few more days. And when she was finally well enough go out for a drive the follow-

---

[25] See Parlby family tree p. 164

17

ing week, "one of the springs of the carriage broke". They all stayed in Colchester until late October when Millie, Blanche and Miss Morton left to go to Folkestone.

This was because Charles took one more trip abroad, this time to Paris with his father. They were able to see all the sights, but Charles was clearly more interested in art than his father. Roger says that he was "very neat with his fingers" and "could draw first-class military sketches". When he went to Burlington House a few months later, and saw the Old Masters Exhibition, he commented that he "liked a few of the pictures very much" and he also visited the National Gallery on a number of occasions. So it is not surprising that, when visiting Versailles, Charles complained that "my father was in such a hurry that I had no time to see the splendid pictures well," and that the same was true when they went to the Louvre where there was the "usual hurry". But they did enjoy dining at the Café de la Paix; seeing *Domino Noir* at the Opera Comique and *Les Monaquetaires* at the Bouffes; and hearing the band of the *Garde Republicaine* at the Palais de l'Industrie.

Millie came to stay again in December when she received a telegram from Manadon announcing the safe arrival of the *Jumna* from India with the Arbuthnotts on board. They went to London and saw her sister Marion and her husband Charles Arbuthnott lunching together at the Grand Hotel. The following day they again went to London from Colchester on an evening train and stayed in St James' Place, seeing Marion and Charles both that evening and for dinner the next night.

Roger's only recollection of living at Colchester at that time "is of the house being decorated for Christmas when, seizing a branch of holly and marching about with it, I knocked a lighted lamp off a wall-bracket, cutting and burning my forehead." His father's diary confirms the incident which took place on Christmas Eve. When he arrived home soon after 8 p.m., he "found Roger had upset a lamp, and cut his forehead badly, close to his right eye".

Charles' domestic arrangements had to be reorganized in January 1881 when the Sawfords, who had been his servants, gave warning of their intention to resign. This led him to "meet the McDonalds by appointment with a view to engaging them as servants. I liked what I saw". The following day he "went down to Dulwich to see the McDonald's late mistress" and had an interview with her. This was clearly satisfactory because in the middle of February he "took over plate and linen from the Sawfords and handed them over to the McDonalds", who were in residence with Miss Morton and two other servants at the time of the census in April.

He also continued to be involved with the general's activities. Early in July he went with the general to Warley to inspect the regimental depot, then on to London and Windsor the next day "for the general volunteer review, which was a great success. More than 52,000 men marched past the Queen." Charles had to arrange for the horses to be sent on ahead and, after the review, he "was busy making out travelling claims for the Windsor review all the morning".

The general carried out regular inspections of troops which Charles had to attend, but the general was also in London or away from the office quite a lot of the time which gave Charles plenty of time for other pursuits. To take the first two weeks in March as an example: in the first week the general was twice out hunting, he inspected a draft of nearly 300 men going to India and when he "didn't go to the office, I stayed at home in the morning". The second week the general went to the cavalry barracks to inspect 100 horses, ordered to go to Natal, and on another occasion "inspected some recruits and 12 more horses for Natal". When he "went to the Hospital", Charles accompanied him, but another day, when Charles "went to the office" he "found the general was not there".

When Charles visited Manadon in June he "walked with Blanche in the garden and then round the village", but on his departure she went to Parke, Bovey Tracey to stay with her stepsister Emily and her husband William Hole. Two months later he "had a sad account of dear Blanche from mother" (Mrs Parlby) and the following day he "was dreadfully shocked at getting a telegram in the morning, to say there was no hope of dear Blanche's recovery." He "telegraphed down for further particulars, and received reply in the afternoon that all was over. She had passed away peacefully and without pain. A great shock." He wrote to Millie and at the end of the week went by train to Mutley for the funeral. "We laid the mortal remains of our dearest Blanche to rest at Pennycross."

By then Charles was only one month from marrying Marian, the eldest daughter of Reverend Hill, rector of Stanway near Colchester where he had moved after being headmaster of Magdalen College

School in Oxford. He built the rectory at Stanway where he lived with his wife, Sarah, whom Roger describes as "a dear old lady", and eight children, four boys and four girls.[26] Roger writes that "my 'mother' (Marian) was the eldest of the four girls; the others were Alice – a lovely, golden-haired girl and tremendous favourite with everybody; Louise, a very good musician, with a twinkle and a very great sense of humour" and Maude, the youngest. "The eldest son was Johnnie, a very clever lad who developed some spinal trouble whilst up at New College and was an invalid at Stanway; Dick, very handsome and popular, in the Royal Irish Constabulary; Quintin was in Australia and Humphry in the Gloucestershire regiment."

The first reference in Charles' diaries to Stanway rectory was in February 1880 when he had lunch there and found the Hills "very pleasant". He dined there again at the beginning of March and found that they had friends in common. But it was the Stanway concert in December that brought him into close contact with the family as he was involved in printing posters, as well as performing. He read *The Taming of the Shrew* with the family which "all the Hills read well"; Dr and Mrs Hill and a younger sister Louise brought over a manuscript of the Stanway concert programme; and in the concert itself he sang two songs and did an encore, staying to dinner afterwards. At the end of December he went with the Hills, they driving in their carriage and Charles riding with Richard Hill to a concert at Coggeshall, where he sang and recited after which he stayed the night at Stanway.

They saw each other frequently in March 1881 after he had returned from his travels to see his father in St Leonards and to Lichfield. He had stayed for an hour and a half at Stanway with "dear Mildred" (Millie) at the end of January which was "very pleasant" and on 8 March his diary entry said that "I wrote to Millie on a subject of great importance". It is very likely that he was telling her of his intentions towards Marian. It is at this time that Marian is first mentioned in his diary, as MH and subsequent entries show his growing feelings for her. When out for a ride three days later, he overtook her on Stanway Hill, and they "had a little chat". The following day, 12 March, was her birthday and he went over to Stanway with Miss Morton and Roger for the afternoon. When "the three boys' birthdays were celebrated", Marian and Alice her sister "very kindly came and I walked back with them. Felt so happy."

---

[26] See Hill family tree p.168

Having gone over to Stanway with Miss Morton and Roger on 9 April and picked primroses, he "had very little time to speak to M, but I think she understands and likes me". Two days later he met Mrs Hill and Marian in London and having discovered that "M is going down by 4.25 tomorrow, I telegraphed the general for leave, and hope to go down with her." When he got to the station he "found M already in a carriage. We came down together and of course the journey was dreadfully soon over. However it was great happiness while it lasted."

Easter Sunday a few days later was "such a happy day for me, but I couldn't say what I longed to do. I must try soon." Two days later "M walked over to the stables with me, but I couldn't say what I wanted to her, and consequently I felt very miserable all night." First thing the next morning, "after a very restless night, I determined I would write to Mrs Hill and tell her all about it" so he did before breakfast before setting out for Aldershot via London where he "chose a wig for M". On his return he "bought a bouquet in Covent Garden, trembling and uncertain whether I should ever give it." But he "had such a nice letter from Mrs Hill" and went to a fancy dress ball at Lexden Park where "I gave the bouquet and was with my darling Marian all night. So happy and thankful. God prosper us!"

Having finally proposed and been accepted he "rode out to Stanway and received most warm congratulations from all the family. They are most kind. Had a jolly time with my darling." He also "told the general and Mrs Radcliffe of my engagement and was so pleased at their liking it so much". He also had "very nice letters from relations giving me good wishes".

However, just as with his first engagement, his financial circumstances again caused him great concern. At the beginning of May he had an interview with Dr Hill "which was satisfactory". His eldest brother William, who had been vital in enabling his wedding to Gertrude to take place, came from London to stay at the end of the month and spent an afternoon at Stanway. Charles was clearly so preoccupied with this problem that "I forgot to order the band for the general's party and caught it in consequence". Things did not seem to be working out and he "felt dreadfully low", made worse when he "had a visit from my father (in London) as I was getting up which made me miserable" leaving him "*fearfully* low".

21

Charles then had to go to Manadon, but his father wrote a note to Mrs Hill which he forwarded. The issue of the marriage settlement clearly still had to be resolved and he only heard from Willie "relative to settlement" just before his departure from Manadon. On his return he had a talk with Dr Hill which he describes as "fairly satisfactory", but at the end of the month he was still writing to Willie and "felt very wretched" when he had had no answer to his letter. Two days later there was still "no letter from Willie which makes me dreadfully anxious", but then he "heard from Willie at last. I'm afraid it won't be very satisfactory, but God grant all may be well!" Fortunately it was and when he had an "interview with Dr Hill on his return from London, he was very kind and I hope all will be right after all. Felt much relieved." Willie seems to have come to the rescue again.

By the beginning of August plans were going ahead for the wedding and Charles "heard from my father and Willie that they would stay here for the wedding. Heard also from Millie." Late in August he "went to the National Gallery with my darling and lunched with her at the grand grill. Then we did some shopping and came down by the 6.20 train." They saw each other every day the following week and arranged the wedding presents in the morning room at Stanway. There was a large garden party at Stanway after which "my darling was dreadfully tired". She was still "very unwell" and, when he arrived for dinner the next day, he found her "nearly dead after a visit from no less than 70 old women!" He drove over to Stanway the following day "to see the presents" and in the evening his father, and Sissie and Arthur Coode arrived. The day before the wedding was the brigade field day, but he was able to delegate his work, meet Willie at the station and dine with him at Stanway in the evening. Thursday, 8 September was their wedding day. Charles went to Stanway for Holy Communion at 8 a.m. and back for breakfast. Then at 10.30 he drove over in General Radcliffe's carriage with his father and Arthur Coode. His sister Sissie and brother Willie went in another carriage. After the wedding the couple left for London by the 2.30 train for their honeymoon.

The honeymoon lasted for a month. They set out from London for Ashbourne spending a few days at the 'Green Man' where they were "so comfortable and lodged so cheaply". A few days later they went to Doncaster for the St Leger when "my darling won 10 shillings." They stayed at Rowsley where they "made the acquaintance of an old clergyman" and had dinner with him two nights running. They enjoyed Matlock, and rowed on the Derwent but went over Haddon Hall "with a horrible guide" and found Chatsworth "rather disappointing". Then to Buxton where they "stayed at a grocer's shop as we couldn't get into the Palace Hotel". After that it was on to Windermere where they went to the Low Wood Hotel "the best I ever stayed in" close to the lake. This enabled them to take a boat out on the lake, see Furness Abbey, Wordsworth's tomb, walk to Kirkstone Pass and have lunch in the "highest house in England". Then on to Derwentwater, walking into Keswick before going to Buttermere, where they "rowed back quietly and read *Pendennis* in the boat". After that it was the Ullswater Hotel "beautiful lake, finest of all". Then on to Edinburgh and the theatre, to Holyrood, St Giles Cathedral and the castle as well as a day trip to Hawthornden "with which we were charmed. The view from Robert Bruce's cave was splendid." They then stopped over at Manchester at the Queen's Hotel which was "very comfortable but frightfully dear. 2/6 and 2/- for two baths". Finally back to London where Dr and Mrs Hill arrived at their hotel and they had an excellent dinner together. Then it was back to Colchester where their married life as a family was about to begin.

CHAPTER THREE

THEATRE AND OTHER INTERESTS

Charles' diaries create a picture of someone who was not just a family man and a soldier, but a talented actor, singer and writer of verses with a wide range of interests. Before moving on to his new married life in Colchester, a look at these other areas provides a fuller understanding of him.

The theatre, in particular, always played a key role in his life. His son Roger records that he "was an excellent actor, and had a lovely singing voice" which he must have inherited from his mother, who was "an excellent musician", and he was in great demand throughout his life to perform in productions, concerts and readings. At the age of 19, while garrisoned at Galway, he played Imogene 'the fair' *par excellence* in *Alonzo the Brave* at the Theatre Royal where in the words of the Galway Vindicator she "was all smiles, sighs, and blushes as the young Faust wooed her". The three-night production was described as achieving "a success for which professionals would have been most grateful". And in a concert the following March, according to the Vindicator, "the comic singing and acting of Mr Mott kept the house in roars of laughter". He certainly made an impact and the same paper reported that the men of the Queen's Regiment present "applauded vociferously – they seem to be proud of him and they have a right to be so" because "it is due to this young officer" that "ever since the detachment of his regiment has been stationed in the town, he has been always ready to give his aid at every entertainment for a charitable purpose".

After his return to England he continued to perform in a variety of concerts and productions, with the Staffordshire Advertiser reporting that his singing was "rapturously applauded". But it was his performance as General Goodwin in *A Hundred Thousand Pounds* that made the greatest impact that night and which "fully bore out his previous high reputation in Lichfield as an actor". This comedy, written by Henry Byron in three acts and first performed at the Prince of Wales's Theatre in 1866, tells of the rival attentions of General Goodwin and Pennythorne, the proprietor of the livery stables, for the chandler's niece Alice.

When Goodwin learns that he is the heir of an uncle who has died in India leaving him £100,000, he forgets his love for Alice although, when his friend insults her, he comes to her defence, with Alice listening in an adjoining room. And, when it turns out that his uncle is not dead but has returned to England, Alice put her small fortune of £4,000 at his disposal. Pennythorne's offer of marriage, in contrast, is based on getting hold of her fortune and when he learns that it has gone, because her uncle is on the verge of ruin, he is enraged. When Goodwin comes to wish them farewell, his plans are changed by a letter from his uncle and the play ends with Goodwin and Alice happily reunited.

This play was performed at a number of venues in the south of England in 1870 and 1871 with Charles playing General Goodwin and his brother Edward, also in the cast, "playing the part of a footman" Pyefinch - "to such perfection", according to one review, that "we are informed that several 'situations' were offered to him in the course of the next day". This was before Edward spent a few years playing strolling parts in productions all around the country. But it was Charles who featured in reviews of the play - the Portsmouth Times said of his performance at the Theatre Royal that his "easy bearing, combined with clear articulation are points which few amateurs can fairly lay claim to; and we must compliment Mr Mott on the possession of both these attainments. His acting throughout was free from staginess". The Hampshire Telegraph said that his "acting in the love scenes with Alice and his expression of remorse for the manner in which, when he becomes rich, he casts her aside, displayed considerable ability" and that he "has attained the enviable power of acting and speaking without restraint before a public audience". And when he played the part of General Goodwin for the 12th time at the Theatre Royal, Exeter in 1872, he showed his "dramatic powers" in a charity performance in front of the Mayor of London.

When Charles married Gertrude and spent time in India he got involved with Arthur Barrow and others in productions there. But it was after her death and his return to England that he threw himself back into the theatre with his appointment at Colchester, a posting which also enabled him to see professional productions in London more frequently. Apart from acting and singing, Charles was also much involved in painting scenery – he was "very neat with his fingers" and could draw "first-class sketches" – and in printing programmes for productions, which, according to Roger, was one of his main hobbies. In December 1881, for example, he printed programmes for entertainments organised by Mildred at Knackersknowle and by her brother Gerald at Felixstowe.

He always set himself high standards when rehearsing - one rehearsal of *Friends or Foes* was "a very bad one and I was very disgusted" but the following afternoon "it went much better". The first performance brought the comment "I was agreeably surprised with it", while the second "was most successful and I was quite pleased afterwards". Productions could also be very time consuming and exhausting, especially when rehearsing two plays at once. The first time that *Lady of Lyons* was rehearsed with "the whole cast at last present" was only four days before the first night and this was a play which had been performed at the Royal Lyceum Theatre in London. Charles had to spend most of the final day at the theatre seeing to the scenery, before performing in front of a good house of about 700 people. The following afternoon there was a rehearsal of *Scrap of Paper* and then "just time to get home and snatch a mouthful of dinner and get back to play *Lady of Lyons*." By this time he was exhausted from being at the office and constant rehearsals, but the final performance of *Scrap of Paper* meant "a rest day at last - no office and no rehearsals". He comments by the end of it all "I was nearly dead".

Rehearsals for another production of *Scrap of Paper* in London with Mrs Crawley, who was a good actress, and Mrs Meares also took up much time and organization and he went with Mrs Crawley to St George's Hall to arrange the performances and to order the programmes to be printed. He also played *Happy Pair* with Mrs Crawley at the Park Theatre in London.

He would willingly take part in all types of concerts and performances. When he was living at Colchester, in particular, he would sing and recite regularly at concerts, with songs such as 'Blue Eyes or Brown Eyes', 'He did and he didn't know why', 'Complaints' and 'Schoolmaster' and recitations such as 'Gemini and Virgo', 'Netley Abbey' and 'The Day of the Nancy Bell'. But the stream of productions put a strain on his health. A two-day Royal Hospital at the Adelphi "a stirring piece with wonderful scenery"; *Confusion* at the Vaudeville "which was immensely funny"; and Mary Anderson in *Lady of Lyons* at the Lyceum "she is pretty and graceful with splendid form. She played the part well but the Claude (Mr Barnes) was execrable". He also had the opportunity of meeting Oscar Wilde who gave two lectures in Colchester and stayed with the Hills at Stanway. "He had tea, rehearsed and dined at our lodgings, 21 Crouch Street. Oscar was most 'intense'. We went in the evening to hear his *Impressions of America*."

Throughout his life Charles composed a number of verses, which he sang at concerts. These were based on a topical song, which he called 'A Quiet Sort of Way', and he added new topical verses for each occasion. The opening verse was:

> With rumours and sensations now the daily papers teem.
> In these days of electricity, machinery and steam.
> I've jotted down a few remarks on topics of the day;
> And I'll tell you all about them, in a quiet sort of way.

The song was performed in Galway in 1868 and, according to the Galway Express, was "so well sung and harmonized so fully with the feelings of an Irish audience that it gained considerable applause, and was *encored*." Later in Dublin in 1875 he introduced some new verses:

> The Dublin Corporation would be surely doing good
> If they paved the City noiselessly, with asphalt or with wood.
> I doubt, though, very much if we shall ever see the day
> When each road will be, like Grafton Street, a quiet sort of way.

> The Dublin Tramway Company is thriving so I hear;
> Fifteen per cent was quoted as their dividend, last year.
> 'Tis very nice to travel, on a pleasant summer day,
> Down to Sandymount for threepence, in a quiet sort of way.

Other verses showed his interest in politics and current affairs. When Charles and Gertrude were sailing to India on 23 February 1878, he sang verses on board HMS *Malabar* in the Indian Ocean. Four of the verses went:

31

We don't feel much excited at the latest news, which tells
That our noble fleet of iron-clads is off the Dardanelles.
We can't forget that once before they made the same display;
Then were sent back to Besika, in a quiet sort of way.

The nation long has had enough of Gladstone's little game,
And the so-called 'Christianity' which Muscovites proclaim.
The peoples' wrath, too long restrained, burst out, the other day,
And they broke the Woodman's windows in no quiet sort of way.

They've passed the recent vote for supplementary supplies
By such a large majority as must have caused surprise.
Sir Stafford, tho', was not afraid; He knew the Country'd pay
The six millions that he asked for, in a quiet sort of way.

Full many a mile from Britain's Isle we've come with rapid steps;
And we've cross'd the Suez Isthmus cut by M. De Lesseps.
Our voyage has been a calm one, and until we reach Bombay
Let us hope the ocean still may prove a quiet sort of way.

These verses show a man who was well-informed about the issues
of the day and who had strong opinions of his own as a staunch
Conservative. The background to the first set of verses is that
Gladstone had condemned Turkish atrocities in Bulgaria and used
every means to mobilize opinion against the Conservative government of Disraeli. Gladstone's 'little game' in verse two was when
he became the reluctant leader of a movement rooted in the non-
conformist congregations of the north and the Anglo-Catholic intel-
lectuals at Oxford. When Russia declared war on Turkey in 1877,
and eventually seemed to threaten Constantinople itself in 1878, public
opinion swung round to support Disraeli and the windows of
Gladstone's house were broken by an anti-Russian mob.

Meanwhile the budget surplus of 1875 had given way to a deficit,
due to economic recession and increased military expenditure, which
is why Sir Stafford Northcote, the Chancellor of the Exchequer, had
to secure extra supplies referred to in verse three.

On 25 November 1880 at Colchester three of the verses that he
sang were:

The present state of Ireland all must view with great alarm.
I don't envy those poor soldiers who are guarding Boycott's farm.
They've all the shifts of warfare to endure and every day
They run the risk of being murdered in a secret sort of way.

Mr Gladstone has assured us that when things go really wrong
He'll not hesitate to stop them with coercion hot and strong.
What crisis he is waiting for I don't pretend to say;
But he daily dilly dallies, in a quiet sort of way.

The secret of a Cabinet will sometimes come to light;
And they say much opposition comes from Chamberlain & Bright.
I think, if I were Gladstone, I should have a word to say
To those Birmingham obstructors, in a quiet sort of way.

In 1880 Gladstone was returned to power and Charles is here being critical of his Irish policy. With problems of land reform unresolved, Parnell urged protests against the government and the landlord class. The Irish 'boycotted' Captain Boycott so that the government was forced to come to his assistance before his crops rotted in the field because no tenant or labourer would work for him. By 1880 there were numerous acts of violence being committed against persons and property, including assault and arson, and Charles bemoans the lack of action by Gladstone over this.

The final verse reflects the role of Chamberlain, president of the Board of Trade and Bright in the cabinet, although Chamberlain was isolated and Bright had lost most of his radical fire.

What comes across strongly in his diaries is his support for the Conservative party. When Disraeli dissolved parliament in March 1880, this proved to be a mistake. On 31 March 1880 Charles wrote that it was "polling day at Colchester and many other boroughs. Colchester disgraced itself by returning two radicals". He reported Radical (Liberal) gains over the next few days but at least "two Conservatives (Round and Brise) were elected for East Essex". Overall though, as he wrote on 8 April, "there is a steady increase in the Radical gain". The overall result was that the Liberals won a convincing victory by 347 seats to 240 Conservatives and the Queen accepted Disraeli's resignation.

When Disraeli (Lord Beaconsfield) fell ill in 1881 Charles followed his progress closely. For example on 7 April "Lord Beaconsfield was worse in the early morning and Sir W. Jenner was called in, but he rallied wonderfully in the afternoon". And on 14 April that he "at last really seems to be picking up a little. Please God he may yet be spared to us, for he is much wanted". And finally on 19 April "very much shocked, on going down to the town after breakfast, to find that Lord Beaconsfield had died at 4.30 this morning". The following year, on the anniversary of his death, Charles was in St Leonards where "nearly everyone wore primroses (his favourite flower)".

He was equally concerned about Gladstone's policy in key areas. With regard to the situation in Ireland, he wrote in October 1881 of the "news of Parnell having been at last arrested. Hope this is the precursor of wise policy on the part of Gladstone's cabinet". But in May 1882 news came "of Lord Cooper and Mr Forster having resigned the Lord Lieutenancy and Chief Secretaryship of Ireland" and of Parnell's liberation. This led to "Lord Frederick Cavendish appointed Chief Secretary for Ireland!!!!" But only two days later "we heard the ghastly news of the murder of Lord Frederick Cavendish and Mr Burke (Chief and Under Secretaries for Ireland) in the Phoenix Park". On the Monday "all the papers full of sickening details of Saturday's assassinations. Parliament only met to adjourn after 20 minutes which was devoted to short expressions of horror and sympathy from all sides". Three days later a "government bill announced for the repression of all crime in Ireland".

Another crisis, which he was close to and had strong views on, was the one which developed in Egypt in 1882. Gladstone's government came under criticism from Charles when he complained about "enforced inactivity on the part of our troops by reason of the inane policy of Gladstone's government". But faced with abandonment of British interests or invasion, Gladstone decided to choose invasion. "Gladstone moved for a vote of credit for Egyptian expedition" which "was voted by an overwhelming majority. Only 19 noes".

All this meant that a large number of troops would need to be sent there. Charles, being based at Aldershot, was in the midst of much activity and over the next few days "the Duke of Cambridge inspected the troops for Egypt on the Queen's Parade; the Life Guards embarked as did the rest of the Household Cavalry; the 50th left Aldershot and the following day "the Queen inspected the 50th on board the *Catalonia* at Portsmouth".

This was to have been a joint expedition with the French but the French government fell and the new ministry withdrew its support. The total British force under Sir Garnet Wolseley was 40,000 troops and Charles followed their progress closely. "One telegram said that 50 wounded had already been brought in. Wolseley telegraphed that the enemy had been repulsed with great loss, we had taken four guns, and our loss was trifling. Very anxious for further particulars". These came when "Sir Garnet (Wolseley) attacked the Egyptian lines at Tel el Kebir before daylight at the point of the bayonet, while the cavalry got round their flank. Total collapse of the Egyptian army. We only lost about 30 killed and 300 wounded". This was followed by the capture of 'Arabi Pasha', who led the Egyptian resistance as a result of which "all was peaceable".

Sir Garnet Wolseley had succeeded in occupying Egypt and Charles wrote of the "grand review of 18,000 British troops at Cairo". He attended a harvest thanksgiving service which was combined with a service "for the success of our armies in Egypt". A month later "the Queen reviewed the whole of the troops at present in England who had returned from Egypt, in London".

Another side of Charles' character can be seen in an entry in his diary at the time of Gertrude's death when he wrote that "it was through my love for her that I first learned to love my Saviour more than I had ever done before". It was also through his love for her that "I trust to continue in the right way and to keep the resolution I have made to devote my future life more entirely to God, and to doing what is right".

His faith was strengthened by his second marriage and his connections with the Hills at Stanway, where he frequently attended services, and he certainly went to church at least twice on Sundays whenever possible.

When he was in London he took the opportunity in February 1882 of attending Westminster Abbey, hearing the anthem and calling on the Dean, and in April he attended the Chapel Royal, Whitehall where he "heard a very good sermon from Dr Baker, headmaster of Merchant Taylor's School", and later in the day went to St Paul's Cathedral "where we heard a splendid sermon from Dr Liddon in which he referred to Mr Darwin" (who had died three days earlier). He would always comment on particular sermons such as that preached by Archdeacon Earle in St John's Church, Weymouth "on progress in religion exemplified by Nicodemus".

When he and Marian were in Lichfield in February 1883 they attended a lecture by Canon Lonsdale on *Early Church History* and then heard him preach in Lichfield Cathedral two days later at the morning service, with the Dean of Lichfield preaching in the afternoon and "a splendid sermon on the 2nd Commandment" from Mr Scott at the evening service at St Mary's. In January 1884 they went to the cathedral to hear *'O rest in the Lord'* and the following day went there in the morning to hear the bishop preach his New Year's sermon, they went with the children in the afternoon to a children's service and Charles went to the evening service at St Mary's with aunt Georgie.

Another place that they enjoyed visiting was Oxford. On one Sunday "we went to morning service at Christ Church Cathedral, where we stayed for Holy Communion" and later went to Magdalen College Chapel for a "beautiful service". Two days later they "went to see the convocation sitting. Rather an interesting debate in which a large number took part", after which they went to New College Chapel.

On a typical Sunday when they were living at Colchester, he went with Marian and Roger and Geoffrey "to morning service at All Saints. We heard a good sermon from the Bishop of Colchester. M and I stayed for Holy Communion. I went to All Saints for evening service. We had selections from *'Christ and His Soldiers'."*

These and many similar entries in his diaries leave one in no doubt of the importance that his faith played in his life and we can now see that he did indeed try for the rest of his life to try to do what he saw to be right.

bazaar meant that he was busy all the previous day putting up the 'Royal Thespian Pavilion'. There were four performances on the first day and no less than six on the second when "during the afternoon there was a tremendous storm which deluged the whole place", followed fortunately by a fine evening. On another occasion two days of recitations and songs in Colchester led to him catching a cold "coming home" and this was later to repeat itself with more serious consequences.

How good an actor was he? He was not a mere amateur enthusiast and he appeared in more professional productions, using the name of C. F. Wilmott. In June 1869 he was at the Royal Olympic Theatre in the Haymarket, London, in a performance directed by Mr Coe, stage director of the theatre, where he received favourable reviews for his role as Sir Frederick Chasemore in *The Dowager.* The following month, directed by Joseph Eldred of the Gaiety Theatre, he performed in *A Rough Diamond* at the Gallery of Illustration in Regent Street. Then in August, as a member of a London company, he appeared in a 12-day run of *Flying Scud* at the Theatre Royal, Portsmouth and the Theatre Royal, Southampton, playing the part of Colonel Mulligan. The following year in August, again using the name of C.F. Wilmott, he was in Portsmouth and Brighton for seven performances of Mr Robertson's comedy *Progress* with the Prince of Wales's Theatre Company. The company had previously performed this play, whose plot "requires only five characters to work it out", at a number of other venues. But for these performances Charles replaced one of the five key actors, with the rest of the cast being "make-weights".

The action takes place at the family seat of Lord Mompesson, the destruction of which is threatened by the railway. Charles appeared as John Ferne, a young and rising civil engineer, making a survey for the proposed railway. He is seen and recognized by Eva, the niece of Lord Mompesson, who loves him rather than the Honourable Arthur Mompesson, played by Edgar Bruce. When Ferne is forbidden the house she has a return of her recent severe illness, which turns out this time to be a matter of the heart. The doctor's prescription is that the young engineer be readmitted to the household and he restores her to perfect health by attaining the consent of her family to their marriage. The Brighton Era described Charles' performance as "exceedingly good", while the Brighton Herald said that he "played the lover in a very quiet and gentlemanly manner.

The more impassioned and telling points were never overstrained; and, altogether, this was a most natural piece of acting".

Edgar Bruce, who played opposite him in *Progress*, and who later became the well-known actor-manager of the Prince of Wales's Theatre in Tottenham Street, felt that Charles was a talented actor. So much so that Roger says that he "wanted my father to leave the army and make the stage his profession, but he would not do that". Bruce, nevertheless, became a great friend of Charles whose diaries show that they often met and dined when he was in London and that Bruce showed him a number of kindnesses. Charles assisted Bruce in February 1880 at the opening performance of *A Little Change* by Sidney Grundy, which he said should be withdrawn as soon as possible, and of *Forget Me Not,* which he found "most interesting" with perfect acting by two or three of the cast, a view confirmed when he saw it again a few weeks later and again in June.

Bruce's most successful production as a theatre manager, was *The Colonel*, a satire on aestheticism written by F.C. Burnard, the editor of Punch and its initial run at the Prince of Wales's Theatre lasted for no less than 550 performances. Sir Squire Bancroft, manager of the Haymarket, brought Burnard the original French version and adaptations and asked him to bring the piece up to date, but decided that he would not stage the play at the Haymarket. The play is based on a well-situated family infiltrated by a religious impostor who threatens to gain control over them and their fortune and is thwarted by the intervention of an old friend - in Burnard's version, an American colonel, after whom the play is named.

At the time Gilbert and Sullivan were also working on an aesthetic subject and it became a matter of timing to prevent *The Colonel* appearing to be a mere imitation. Edgar Bruce took the risk and accepted the play which came out in February 1881 just in time to become firmly established before Gilbert and Sullivan's *Patience* opened in April. When Charles saw *Patience* he said that it was "the greatest rot I have seen for a long time. It required a great amount of patience on my part to sit it out".

But he loved *The Colonel* which he saw on a number of occasions. He dined with Bruce and went to the second night which he found "most amusing" and commented "I feel sure it will be a success". And it *was* - he dined with Bruce again a few weeks later and "went to the Prince of Wales where they are doing splendid business". *The Colonel* was so successful that Bruce set up a second company to tour the provinces with the production with Bruce himself playing the part of the colonel. In May 1881 Charles saw a matinee at the Prince of Wales and two days later met Bruce and *The Colonel* touring company at Colchester station prior to a performance, in which Herbert Beerbohm Tree played Lambert Streyke, a part which he subsequently played at the Prince's. The play "was a great success", and after the performance "Bruce and Mrs Crawley (who was also in the cast) dined with me. Didn't get to bed till 4 o'clock".

Then, while they were in Edinburgh on honeymoon at the start of October, Charles and Marian discovered that the touring company was performing *The Colonel* at the Theatre Royal, where they "met Bruce who gave us a very good box". They also learnt that the Prince of Wales had persuaded his mother, Queen Victoria, to call off her mourning for Prince Albert to see this satire on aestheticism, the first performance she had attended since 1859. Three days later, on Tuesday 4 October, the company put on a special performance for her at Abergeldie Castle, using an improvised stage and watched by 200 guests. When the Queen arrived from nearby Balmoral at nine o'clock, accompanied by the Prince and Princess of Wales and Princess Beatrice, the Queen's attendants and gillies carried torches, while an enormous bonfire opposite the entrance lit up the surrounding hills. Bruce presented the Queen with a nosegay and play bill before the performance and she spoke to him at the end. The *Whitehall Review* commented that no-one in the room "saw the points or responded to them with such hearty laughter as the Queen" and she herself wrote that she *had* "been most amused"![27] The cast were then entertained to supper by the Prince of Wales until 2 a.m. It had been a great night for Edgar Bruce.

Charles and Marian saw *The Colonel* again at the Prince of Wales in London the following February and a few days later Bruce brought his touring company down to put on *The Colonel* at the Colchester Theatre for two nights before moving on to Cambridge. All this success with *The Colonel* made Edgar Bruce a handsome profit and he decided to build a new theatre from the proceeds. This new Prince's Theatre was built in Coventry Street and was flowery in style with a Moorish foyer, with a fountain playing, and a 'smok-

---

[27] Theatre Museum THM/57 – Tonie Edgar Bruce Collection

ing fernery' and 'grotto' complete with ornamental rocks beneath. Inside was a traditional three-tier theatre, decorated with white, cream and gold that seated more than 1,000 people. Stronger colours of burnt orange and terracotta were used for the drapes and seats.[28]

In November 1883 Charles and Marian first met Bruce in his "new Prince's Theatre and he showed us all over it". He said that it was "a grand building and I hope it may be a success". Bruce again benefited from the Prince of Wales' patronage receiving a royal grant to allow the theatre to bear his name and to use the Prince of Wales' feathers. When Bruce formally opened his new theatre on Friday 18 January 1884 in the presence of the Prince of Wales, with *Palace of Truth* starring Herbert Beerbohm Tree, and *In Honour Bound*, Charles was away in Ireland. But he was back in London at the beginning of March and went to see *Breaking a Butterfly* at the Prince's which he described as a "lovely theatre but rotten piece". He was given another tour by Bruce going "all over the theatre", but found him "very low about the Prince's" because of the problems of finding the right productions. A week later he "gave us a box at the Prince's", but the choice of plays continued to be a problem and, when Charles went to see the first night of *The Private Secretary*, he found it "very boisterous, but no lasting power, I fear". However, when Bruce again gave them a box at the Prince's to see *Called Back*, Charles felt that it was a "real strong play with good situations. Well mounted and acted" and four months later, when he saw it again, it was still going strong.

Charles never seems to have missed an opportunity to go to the theatre when he visited London and frequently comments on the productions that he saw. He had mixed opinions of Henry Irving, manager of the Lyceum Theatre. In November 1880 he went to the *Corsican Brothers* at the Lyceum "very good, but for Irving's mannerisms". But in April 1882 he saw *Romeo and Juliet* and found "Irving too killing as the *antique* hero. The scenery and appointments were perfect". The following February he saw *Much Ado About Nothing* commenting that "Ellen Terry was splendid" and "Irving better than usual".

In November 1883 he and Marian saw *Fedora* at the Haymarket where 'Bancroft's burlesque of 'Louis' was 'too too''; *In the Ranks*

---

[28] There is almost nothing left of Bruce's theatre, apart from one wall which allowed the actors to walk under the stage. Otherwise it has been completely rebuilt.

at the Adelphi "a stirring piece with wonderful scenery"; *Confusion* at the Vaudeville "which was immensely funny"; and Mary Anderson in *Lady of Lyons* at the Lyceum "she is pretty and graceful with splendid form. She played the part well but the Claude (Mr Barnes) was execrable". He also had the opportunity of meeting Oscar Wilde who gave two lectures in Colchester and stayed with the Hills at Stanway. "He had tea, rehearsed and dined at our lodgings, 21 Crouch Street. Oscar was most 'intense'. We went in the evening to hear his *Impressions of America.*"

Throughout his life Charles composed a number of verses, which he sang at concerts. These were based on a topical song, which he called 'A Quiet Sort of Way', and he added new topical verses for each occasion. The opening verse was:

> With rumours and sensations now the daily papers teem.
> In these days of electricity, machinery and steam.
> I've jotted down a few remarks on topics of the day;
> And I'll tell you all about them, in a quiet sort of way.

The song was performed in Galway in 1868 and, according to the Galway Express, was "so well sung and harmonized so fully with the feelings of an Irish audience that it gained considerable applause, and was *encored*." Later in Dublin in 1875 he introduced some new verses:

> The Dublin Corporation would be surely doing good
> If they paved the City noiselessly, with asphalt or with wood.
> I doubt, though, very much if we shall ever see the day
> When each road will be, like Grafton Street, a quiet sort of way.

> The Dublin Tramway Company is thriving so I hear;
> Fifteen per cent was quoted as their dividend, last year.
> 'Tis very nice to travel, on a pleasant summer day,
> Down to Sandymount for threepence, in a quiet sort of way.

Other verses showed his interest in politics and current affairs. When Charles and Gertrude were sailing to India on 23 February 1878, he sung verses on board HMS *Malabar* in the Indian Ocean. Four of the verses went:

31

We don't feel much excited at the latest news, which tells
That our noble fleet of iron-clads is off the Dardanelles.
We can't forget that once before they made the same display;
Then were sent back to Besika, in a quiet sort of way.

The nation long has had enough of Gladstone's little game,
And the so-called 'Christianity' which Muscovites proclaim.
The peoples' wrath, too long restrained, burst out, the other day,
And they broke the Woodman's windows in no quiet sort of way.

They've passed the recent vote for supplementary supplies
By such a large majority as must have caused surprise.
Sir Stafford, tho', was not afraid; He knew the Country'd pay
The six millions that he asked for, in a quiet sort of way.

Full many a mile from Britain's Isle we've come with rapid steps;
And we've cross'd the Suez Isthmus cut by M. De Lesseps.
Our voyage has been a calm one, and until we reach Bombay
Let us hope the ocean still may prove a quiet sort of way.

These verses show a man who was well-informed about the issues
of the day and who had strong opinions of his own as a staunch
Conservative. The background to the first set of verses is that
Gladstone had condemned Turkish atrocities in Bulgaria and used
every means to mobilize opinion against the Conservative government of Disraeli. Gladstone's 'little game' in verse two was when
he became the reluctant leader of a movement rooted in the non-
conformist congregations of the north and the Anglo-Catholic intel-
lectuals at Oxford. When Russia declared war on Turkey in 1877,
and eventually seemed to threaten Constantinople itself in 1878, public
opinion swung round to support Disraeli and the windows of
Gladstone's house were broken by an anti-Russian mob.

Meanwhile the budget surplus of 1875 had given way to a deficit,
due to economic recession and increased military expenditure, which
is why Sir Stafford Northcote, the Chancellor of the Exchequer, had
to secure extra supplies referred to in verse three.

On 25 November 1880 at Colchester three of the verses that he
sang were:

The present state of Ireland all must view with great alarm.
I don't envy those poor soldiers who are guarding Boycott's farm.
They've all the shifts of warfare to endure and every day
They run the risk of being murdered in a secret sort of way.

Mr Gladstone has assured us that when things go really wrong
He'll not hesitate to stop them with coercion hot and strong.
What crisis he is waiting for I don't pretend to say;
But he daily dilly dallies, in a quiet sort of way.

The secret of a Cabinet will sometimes come to light;
And they say much opposition comes from Chamberlain & Bright.
I think, if I were Gladstone, I should have a word to say
To those Birmingham obstructors, in a quiet sort of way.

In 1880 Gladstone was returned to power and Charles is here being critical of his Irish policy. With problems of land reform unresolved, Parnell urged protests against the government and the landlord class. The Irish 'boycotted' Captain Boycott so that the government was forced to come to his assistance before his crops rotted in the field because no tenant or labourer would work for him. By 1880 there were numerous acts of violence being committed against persons and property, including assault and arson, and Charles bemoans the lack of action by Gladstone over this.

The final verse reflects the role of Chamberlain, president of the Board of Trade and Bright in the cabinet, although Chamberlain was isolated and Bright had lost most of his radical fire.

What comes across strongly in his diaries is his support for the Conservative party. When Disraeli dissolved parliament in March 1880, this proved to be a mistake. On 31 March 1880 Charles wrote that it was "polling day at Colchester and many other boroughs. Colchester disgraced itself by returning two radicals". He reported Radical (Liberal) gains over the next few days but at least "two Conservatives (Round and Brise) were elected for East Essex". Overall though, as he wrote on 8 April, "there is a steady increase in the Radical gain". The overall result was that the Liberals won a convincing victory by 347 seats to 240 Conservatives and the Queen accepted Disraeli's resignation.

When Disraeli (Lord Beaconsfield) fell ill in 1881 Charles followed his progress closely. For example on 7 April "Lord Beaconsfield was worse in the early morning and Sir W. Jenner was called in, but he rallied wonderfully in the afternoon". And on 14 April that he "at last really seems to be picking up a little. Please God he may yet be spared to us, for he is much wanted". And finally on 19 April "very much shocked, on going down to the town after breakfast, to find that Lord Beaconsfield had died at 4.30 this morning". The following year, on the anniversary of his death, Charles was in St Leonards where "nearly everyone wore primroses (his favourite flower)".

He was equally concerned about Gladstone's policy in key areas. With regard to the situation in Ireland, he wrote in October 1881 of the "news of Parnell having been at last arrested. Hope this is the precursor of wise policy on the part of Gladstone's cabinet". But in May 1882 news came "of Lord Cooper and Mr Forster having resigned the Lord Lieutenancy and Chief Secretaryship of Ireland" and of Parnell's liberation. This led to "Lord Frederick Cavendish appointed Chief Secretary for Ireland!!!!" But only two days later "we heard the ghastly news of the murder of Lord Frederick Cavendish and Mr Burke (Chief and Under Secretaries for Ireland) in the Phoenix Park". On the Monday "all the papers full of sickening details of Saturday's assassinations. Parliament only met to adjourn after 20 minutes which was devoted to short expressions of horror and sympathy from all sides". Three days later a "government bill announced for the repression of all crime in Ireland".

Another crisis, which he was close to and had strong views on, was the one which developed in Egypt in 1882. Gladstone's government came under criticism from Charles when he complained about "enforced inactivity on the part of our troops by reason of the inane policy of Gladstone's government". But faced with abandonment of British interests or invasion, Gladstone decided to choose invasion. "Gladstone moved for a vote of credit for Egyptian expedition" which "was voted by an overwhelming majority. Only 19 noes".

All this meant that a large number of troops would need to be sent there. Charles, being based at Aldershot, was in the midst of much activity and over the next few days "the Duke of Cambridge inspected the troops for Egypt on the Queen's Parade; the Life Guards embarked as did the rest of the Household Cavalry; the 50th left Aldershot and the following day "the Queen inspected the 50th on board the *Catalonia* at Portsmouth".

This was to have been a joint expedition with the French but the French government fell and the new ministry withdrew its support. The total British force under Sir Garnet Wolseley was 40,000 troops and Charles followed their progress closely. "One telegram said that 50 wounded had already been brought in. Wolseley telegraphed that the enemy had been repulsed with great loss, we had taken four guns, and our loss was trifling. Very anxious for further particulars". These came when "Sir Garnet (Wolseley) attacked the Egyptian lines at Tel el Kebir before daylight at the point of the bayonet, while the cavalry got round their flank. Total collapse of the Egyptian army. We only lost about 30 killed and 300 wounded". This was followed by the capture of 'Arabi Pasha', who led the Egyptian resistance as a result of which "all was peaceable".

Sir Garnet Wolseley had succeeded in occupying Egypt and Charles wrote of the "grand review of 18,000 British troops at Cairo". He attended a harvest thanksgiving service which was combined with a service "for the success of our armies in Egypt". A month later "the Queen reviewed the whole of the troops at present in England who had returned from Egypt, in London".

Another side of Charles' character can be seen in an entry in his diary at the time of Gertrude's death when he wrote that "it was through my love for her that I first learned to love my Saviour more than I had ever done before". It was also through his love for her that "I trust to continue in the right way and to keep the resolution I have made to devote my future life more entirely to God, and to doing what is right".

His faith was strengthened by his second marriage and his connections with the Hills at Stanway, where he frequently attended services, and he certainly went to church at least twice on Sundays whenever possible.

When he was in London he took the opportunity in February 1882 of attending Westminster Abbey, hearing the anthem and calling on the Dean, and in April he attended the Chapel Royal, Whitehall where he "heard a very good sermon from Dr Baker, headmaster of Merchant Taylor's School", and later in the day went to St Paul's Cathedral "where we heard a splendid sermon from Dr Liddon in which he referred to Mr Darwin" (who had died three days earlier). He would always comment on particular sermons such as that preached by Archdeacon Earle in St John's Church, Weymouth "on progress in religion exemplified by Nicodemus".

When he and Marian were in Lichfield in February 1883 they attended a lecture by Canon Lonsdale on *Early Church History* and then heard him preach in Lichfield Cathedral two days later at the morning service, with the Dean of Lichfield preaching in the afternoon and "a splendid sermon on the 2nd Commandment" from Mr Scott at the evening service at St Mary's. In January 1884 they went to the cathedral to hear *'O rest in the Lord'* and the following day went there in the morning to hear the bishop preach his New Year's sermon, they went with the children in the afternoon to a children's service and Charles went to the evening service at St Mary's with aunt Georgie.

Another place that they enjoyed visiting was Oxford. On one Sunday "we went to morning service at Christ Church Cathedral, where we stayed for Holy Communion" and later went to Magdalen College Chapel for a "beautiful service". Two days later they "went to see the convocation sitting. Rather an interesting debate in which a large number took part", after which they went to New College Chapel.

On a typical Sunday when they were living at Colchester, he went with Marian and Roger and Geoffrey "to morning service at All Saints. We heard a good sermon from the Bishop of Colchester. M and I stayed for Holy Communion. I went to All Saints for evening service. We had selections from *'Christ and His Soldiers'.*"

These and many similar entries in his diaries leave one in no doubt of the importance that his faith played in his life and we can now see that he did indeed try for the rest of his life to try to do what he saw to be right.

CHAPTER FOUR

CHARLES AND MARIAN

On their return to Colchester after their honeymoon in October 1881, Charles and Marian were initially very busy unpacking and arranging wedding presents. A few days later they went to London where they "had a long day at the stores and met the children at Paddington" off the train from Manadon and brought them down to Colchester. There was a change of nurse for the children – Fanny left and Mary Merritt arrived. She was to become a key member of the household for several years and was paid £5-5-0 per quarter, together with her beer money of 13/- a month. The McDonalds continued to keep house for them. They also had a groom Farmfield, paid 18/- a week, and this enabled Charles and Marian to pay social calls in the afternoons after Charles' work at the office in the mornings. On one particularly busy day Marian's brother "Richard came to lunch" after which "we called on Robinsons, Howards, Holly Trees, East Hill House and Greigs (all in) and Grey Friars (out). Reggie came up in afternoon. We dined at Lexden Park. Very pleasant evening."

The children were increasingly involved in their lives as well. Roger accompanied Marian to Stanway for lunch and then went with both of them to an afternoon service the next day, while Geoffrey went for lunch with them to Stanway a few weeks later. When Charles' father, William, came to stay the night in November 1881, he was able to see the fireworks with the children the following day before leaving on the 9.20 train. The following February when Marian wrote to him for his 67th birthday, Roger enclosed a letter for him.

Stanway featured largely in their lives with visits to and from Marian's parents, Dr and Mrs Hill, and her sisters Alice and Louise. Roger remembers Alice as "lovely with magnificent auburn hair" and Louise as "small, very musical, and twinkling with amusement". They "were as good as curates to their father, knowing everyone in the village, and running the choir." They also visited Grey Friars frequently to see the General and his wife, for example on 2 December when it was the general's birthday.

However, their social life was soon curtailed because Marian was "not feeling at all well" and on 9 December "my darling wife was ordered to lie down for a few days". Five days later she still had "to keep to her room" and by 16 December he wrote that "my darling has to stay in bed entirely for some time". But she still had a number of visitors that day as her mother came and sat with her as did her sister Alice and the general's wife, Mrs Radcliffe. When Charles had to be away in Felixstowe overnight Alice came to stay with her sister. On Boxing Day they were "busy all morning dressing the Christmas tree" and eight visitors "were present at our tree" and although "my darling couldn't come down" she "received all visitors in her bedroom".

Charles' eldest brother, Willie, came to stay on New Year's Eve and remained until 5 January when he left for London, but, apart from being carried downstairs briefly on a stretcher on two occasions, Marian was confined to her room. "My darling was to have come downstairs" on Tuesday 10 January but "she had so many visitors that she was too tired". It was not until the next day that he was finally able to move "my darling down stairs at last for luncheon" – she had been up in her room for nearly a month.

The doctor, Mr Worts, "came to see my darling" on the Saturday and "gave his consent to her moving to Stanway. We started about 4.30 in the Stanway carriage and driving slowly reached there in about an hour. My darling bore the journey very well, thank God, though of course she was tired after it, and went to bed soon after she had arrived." All was well when Mr Worts saw her a few days later.

The cause of this long confinement was the early stages of pregnancy but when "Mr Worts came to see my darling" on 25 January he said that he "should not call again as she was doing so well". They were able to walk as far as the Stanway schoolroom on 3 February when they showed the schoolchildren "the bracelet they had given her as a wedding present".

Life at Colchester, with Charles working for the general, suited them all well and helped them to settle down as a family. Charles helped to dress a Christmas tree at Grey Friars on 17 January when there was a children's party there in the afternoon. They took Roger and Geoffrey to the Theatre on 4 March to see *Hamilton's Pan-*

orama. They celebrated all three boys' birthdays on Geoffrey's fourth birthday, 23 March, with Daisy Walker and Percy Radcliffe coming to tea with them. General and Mrs Radcliffe came afterwards, although "my darling was very tired after the exertions with the children".

Marian was also close to her family at Stanway and Charles was able to rehearse and perform frequently in local concerts and productions and to get up to London to go to the theatre. They were both able to go to London at the beginning of February when they visited Westminster Abbey and were introduced to the dean and shown round the deanery. They also did some shopping and saw a number of productions. They also continued their social activities in Colchester for example attending an 'at home' at Mrs George Round's – the wife of the local MP for East Essex - on 15 March.

However, on 22 February he learnt that his life was to change again because a new general had been appointed, Sir H Clifford. He was no longer to be *Aide-de-Camp* (ADC) and on 4 March when he went to the office "my successor, Major Hemming, arrived and I took him about and showed him Grey Friars". Charles had to rejoin his regiment and heard from the general on 11 March that "most likely I should be appointed to the second battalion" (rather than the first as he expected). He commented that he was "rather disgusted". He "went to the office for the last time" on 30 March, "said goodbye to all there and cleared out all my possessions. The new ADC Hemming was there." The following day "we went to see the general off". Charles wrote that he was "very sorry to part" from General Radcliffe. "It seems very strange to be cut adrift again." By 3 April they were all busy packing up their things.

The children travelled to Manadon on 11 April and the following day the heavy baggage was sent on from their house, bills were paid to different tradesmen and the McDonalds departed. Charles and Marian made the most of a period of extended leave over the next month to catch up with friends and relations. They went to London where they met up with Charles' brother, Willie, before going on to his father at St Leonards. Unfortunately Marian was "very much shaken" by a drive with his father in the brougham and, for the next two days, Charles paid for a bath chair to take her to Hastings.

They had joined up with the children at Manadon on 25 April where they saw Mr and Mrs Parlby and Millie. While they were staying there, there was a "perfect cyclone" with several trees being blown down and a few days later Charles wrote "I amused myself by chopping up a horse chestnut tree which was broken in two by the gale." Mr Parlby was involved with the Board of Guardians at Plympton and the asylum at Exminster, but he was also a keen sailor and took Charles out on his boat at Newton Ferrers, near Plymouth. After paying the servants at Manadon 10/-, Charles and Marian left to stay for a few days with his sister Sissie and her husband, Arthur Coode at their house in St Austell in Cornwall, while the children stayed behind at Manadon, and after that they went with Roger to the Holes at Parke, Bovey Tracey where they had two days otter hunting.

While at Parke they also spent a day trying to find somewhere to live in Dawlish. On 22 May the family was reunited in Dawlish where they were housed at 10 Marine Parade for £3-13-6 a week. But Charles got another shock on 28 May because he "had official intimation that I had been given leave (unsolicited) to 15 September at which time I should be ready to embark for India to join the second battalion." He was "completely taken aback as by right I ought to belong to the first battalion", which was not destined for India. With memories of his previous posting to India with Gertrude and the prospects that this one would mean for his family, he must have been much relieved on 6 June when a fellow officer, Collis, offered to exchange battalions with him if he paid him £200, a sum, nevertheless, which would not be easy to raise.

Meanwhile they were able to spend time in Dawlish together as a family. They "took the children out in a boat in the morning to some distant sands and bathed them" on 30 May, while in the afternoon my darling and I went by train to Teignmouth and went out in a boat on the Teign" which they found "very pleasant". On other days Charles walked to Exeter (12½ miles) and came back by train; went by train to Newton Abbot, walked to Torquay where he attended a meeting of the Salvation Army, at which General Booth spoke, then walked on to Teignmouth and back by train; and walked to Parke via Ideford and Chudleigh.

They left the children behind at Dawlish with their nurses on 19 June and set out for Salisbury and then Aldershot. There they met up with Collis and, after lunching with him, Charles wrote to Colonel Hevey "about our exchange". Both Charles and Collis "were medically examined" on 30 June "for our exchange of battalions". In the event the exchange did take place, as Charles put it "a sacrifice of nearly £150 added to a most generous gift of £100 from Arthur Coode saved our going to India. I hope I did right." Charles now went up to camp and joined the first battalion.

Of more immediate consequence, on the day that he wrote to Colonel Hevey, Marian "felt unwell and I made her go to bed", sending for Dr Barker. She continued in pain all night, during which I sat up with her and we got a Mrs Lemon to come in. It was evident that she was on the eve of her confinement and on 23 June at about 5.30 a.m. I went again for Dr Barker, who came about six, and remained with my darling till she was safely delivered of a daughter at about 9.50 a.m." Charles proclaimed himself "so happy and so delighted at the sex". Both mother and daughter were "doing splendidly". Charles paid for the chloroform that had been used and bought a feeding cup for the baby. He then sent telegrams to Mrs Hill and Mrs Hughes (the nurse who had been engaged from Oxford). "The former arrived at about 2 o'clock and the latter about 7.45 p.m., Mrs Lemon having done all that was necessary beforehand." He wrote a lot of letters and concluded "we have indeed much to be thankful for".

All continued to go well and, with Marian and the baby in safe hands, Charles was able to go to London to meet Dr Hill and Alice and go with them to Lord's three days running to see the Oxford v Cambridge match. Charles then had to arrange rooms for the children and nurses in Aldershot, presumably so that they would not prove too much for Marian and the baby. When the children arrived from Dawlish three days later, they stayed at 7 Cyprus Villas and it wasn't until the next day that "the boys came up to see their mother". Charles then returned to Stanway to collect some of their plate and their two dogs, Puck and Tatters, who took time to adapt to their new surroundings because the next day "I lost the dogs in the afternoon but they turned up again".

Marian and the baby continued to thrive but, on 11 July when Charles was due to go to Lord's to see the MCC v the Australians, the child was not very well so he did not go. The next day because she was still not well and they were concerned about her "we had her baptized 'Gertrude Alice'." Fortunately she quickly improved and Charles was able to go to Lord's for two days with Collis to see the Eton v Harrow match.

The day of 18 July was important, Dr Hill and Alice arrived, the whole family moved into 7 Cyprus Villas and most importantly "our little darling was received into the church". She was named Gertrude Alice after Charles' first wife and he writes touchingly "may she grow up in the steps of my darling after whom she is named". The following day all was well enough for Mrs Hill and the nurse to leave, but Alice stayed on with them, going for walks with Roger and Geoffrey and going to the Aldershot races with Charles.

Mr and Mrs Parlby arrived on 1 August after staying at General Radcliffe's. They clearly got on well with the children – Roger and Geoffrey went for a walk with their father and Mr Parlby while, on another day, the children drove with Mrs Parlby to Farnborough while Charles and Marian went to look at 4 Lorne Villas.

Charles had, meanwhile, resumed his regimental duties. He was brigade and regimental captain on 6 August and took the Roman Catholics of the brigade to church. The following day he sat on a board of examination for volunteer officers of the first Hants, two days later sat in on a court martial and the next day went up to camp for early drill. Meanwhile troops were leaving all the time for Egypt.

They moved from their lodgings to their new house, 4 Lorne Villas, on 14 August at a rent of £9-9-0 a month and more of their things arrived from Colchester, but four days later he suddenly heard that there was "a report current that we are to move to Portland next week". This proved to be correct as the next day "the orders arrived for us to go to Portland on Friday next". This again meant a major domestic upheaval. Two days before Charles was due to go to Portland "Mildred was to have come to us but never appeared, nor was there a line from her in explanation". Charles "went to meet Mildred by the 7.43 train" the following day, "but she never came". Fortunately "in the middle of dinner Mildred arrived, very tired, having come all the way from Yorkshire."

He said goodbye to his wife and children on 25 August and went up to camp where the regiment paraded in pouring rain with the result that "we were as wet as possible by the time we reached the station". When he reached Portland he was "not much impressed with the look of the place". The next day he found his baggage at the station and the heavy baggage also came over - he then went over to Weymouth and did some house hunting.

Portland was a miserable billet and he was most unimpressed by the entertainment available in the area. The Weymouth Races were "as poor a performance as I ever saw" while a visit to the theatre provoked the comment "whether the building or the performance was the more wretched would be an open question". He also had problems finding a house – when he went to look at one he couldn't get in. There was "such a thick sea fog with drizzling rain" on 1 September "as would have made any place look miserable, therefore our convict settlement did not show to advantage". He describes it as "one of the most wretched days I ever knew". He was concerned that he might have to live in the barracks in charge of a detachment and continued his search for a house which still proved elusive. He looked at a house on the Dorchester Road "which did not suit", but then fortunately found one that would do and "agreed to take Mrs Drake's house, 3 Prospect Place", for £7-10-0 a month.

A week later he went back to Aldershot to pack up and collect the family and they all finally arrived in Portland on 14 September and went to live in Prospect Place. As he put it with understandable feeling "may we be happy there, and not have to move again for some little time", although it was certainly not where he would have chosen to be posted or to have lived. But the next few days were busy with "putting things to rights" – one afternoon was taken up with putting up pictures and "the writing table arrived from Hawkes and Freeman's". They also attended an auction sale and bought a few things and the man came to tune the piano. Meanwhile the children went by train to Weymouth and had a day on the sands. Mary was still with them and they "took Burrowes as servant" for 15/- a month. The following month Lizzie the nursery maid came and stayed until the following June.

Life now settled into a new pattern. Charles' duties at the barracks were not arduous, enabling both of them to receive and make calls, to go for walks, or on trips into Weymouth to go shopping or go to the dentist. In the middle of October Charles "had an encounter with Scriven, a butcher, who complained of depredations on the part of Puck" (his dog). There is an entry in his accounts of 1/- "for Puck's misdemeanour" but it is crossed out and he wrote 'refused'! He had referred the issue to a solicitor and when the case came to the County Court "I won without any trouble". The same day he had some other good news: "a windfall in the shape of a cheque for £5-9-11, a residuum of the Kynaston Estate. I find thereby I am £79 richer than I thought." This must refer to the estate of his uncle, Roger Kynaston, who was a well-known cricketer and secretary to the MCC at Lord's. Charles' brother, Edward, says that Roger

Kynaston "collected the money necessary to purchase the freehold of Lord's". He was also a Poor Law Guardian for the parish of Marylebone, and chairman of the Greenwich Railway Company. He clearly had considerable business acumen and, according to Edward, he was their father William's "principal adviser", and "was always looked up to as the business member of the family".[29] He died in 1874 and left his property to Edward's elder brother Willie, but Charles must also have benefited in a small way.[30]

Life at Portland continued to be unexciting, although it had its moments. In November "Private Ede cut his throat in the billiard room of the sergeants' mess – a ghastly sight. He still lives however." And two days later Charles had to hold a board in hospital on a man who "had broken two fingers and cut off a third while carrying a drum of paint, weighing 140 lbs".

Charles had to spend time in the officers' mess and his bills for the months of October, November and December amounted to £16-4-1. He also got involved in local entertainments at the end of the year which meant painting scenery and putting on productions. There were plenty of opportunities for social calls. The boys "spent the day" with Lily Mackie while the parents saw a lot of the Rusbridgers, as well as paying a number of other visits. Willie stayed for a few days over Christmas, but when they "went to the barracks for Xmas dinners" he described them as "the most miserable specimens I have ever seen".

They were able to get away from Portland at the beginning of January. The boys were sent off by train to Manadon from Yeovil Junction and by 8 January Charles and Marian were in London and able to shop, dine out and go to the theatre again for the next five nights, something that they must have really appreciated after being cut off in Portland.

Then it was off to Stanway for nearly a month which included preparations for the Stanway concert as well as visits to Colchester and walks with Marian's sisters Alice, Louise and the youngest Maude

---

[29] *A Mingled Yarn* p. 5
[30] Charles' grandfather, John Mott, had married Henrietta Oakeley and her sister Georgina had married Roger Kynaston. Their son, also named Roger, is the Kynaston referred to here and, having no children, he left his property to Charles' brother William. See Kynaston family tree p. 166

and her brothers Richard and Humphry, who had recently had typhoid fever. Then back to London for a few days where they saw Willie, went to more productions and visited the National Gallery before setting out for St Leonards and a visit to his father for a few days before returning briefly to London *en route* to Lichfield where they "had a hearty welcome" from aunts Emily and Georgiana. They also went to Wall on a couple of occasions, having lunch and tea with the Stokes at the vicarage, and visited "the old house in the (cathedral) Close (Lichfield) which I had not been in since my grandfather's death, now 14 years ago." The whole visit to Lichfield was described as "most pleasant".

After that they went to Oxford where they saw the varsity sports, went to services at Christ Church Cathedral and Magdalen Chapel and looked at New College Chapel, lunched at Exeter College, and Magdalen College, and dined at St John's and visited New College, St Mary Hall and Magdalen College School. They also heard a "very tame debate" on the Affirmation Bill at the Oxford Union.

When they travelled back to Portland on 10 March, they had been away for two months and were "very glad to be home" and reunited as a family. On the way they met up with Mary, Maude and the baby and Charles picked up the three boys from Yeovil Junction station on their return from Manadon, supervised by Reginald Parlby, a few days later. Two days later, on Louis' fourth birthday, they kept all three boys' birthdays as usual with Lily Mackie and another girl spending the afternoon and having tea with them. Roger was shortly to be six and Geoffrey five.

There were some benefits to being in Portland, most of them naval. Just after Easter ten members of the regiment went on board the *Hercules* for the day. "We steamed out about eight miles and had some target practice. Two Electric broadsides, each from four 18 ton ML Guns. Altogether 64 rounds were expended, ending by blowing up the target with a torpedo on the end of a boom." On shore he had some instruction in Watkins' 'Range Finder' and later that year the whole company had its course in musketry firing mainly on the Chesil Beach range.

In April he sent in an application to become an adjutant of auxiliary forces, which would have been a more rewarding appointment, but a week later he "heard from Colonel Blake of the Hertfordshire Volunteers that several of the 16th officers wanted the appointment of volunteer adjutant, so I have no chance of it." He did have an interview with General Elkington but felt that it was "not very successful".

Maude stayed until mid-April when Dr Hill came to join his youngest daughter for a few days. By now Charles and Marian had developed a much wider social circle and there were many more visits to make. The Rusbridgers still featured strongly and at the end of April they went with them to Wareham, walked by Corfe Castle to Swanage and then took the boat to Bournemouth and then back by train. Two days later Charles and Marian took Roger and Geoffrey out to pick wild flowers, but Louis and the baby were "both very seedy with coughs. I hope nothing serious is going to happen." Fortunately they were "decidedly better" the following day. Two days later Geoffrey "had his tonsils cut by Dr McLean. He bore the operation wonderfully well." Charles and Marian then went to the Isle of Wight for a few days where they were reunited with Dr Hill and Maude. While at Shanklin "we went to a service at St Saviour's on the Cliff, the same church where seven years ago I had worshipped with my precious Gertrude." He had recently sent a cheque to the Reverend Hardy in Malta for £2-0-0, presumably for the continued care of her grave.

On their return to Portland, Alice Hill came to stay and, while she was there, "we drove in for the yeomanry ball in an omnibus" which was "a fearful journey. Poor Alice Haddon was so knocked up that she couldn't dance, but had to lie down all the time. The others went back by the same conveyance." Charles had to bring back Alice Haddon on the train. Geoffrey remembers a more colourful version that "his father, for lack of anything more commodious, chartered a 'black maria' to convey the ladies of the regiment to a ball."

The next few months saw a succession of visitors: Sissie and Arthur Coode, Miss Morton, Mr Parlby and Mildred. But at the end of June Charles "heard that my company was to be the next to go through the six weeks course, so I applied for leave to go up to London" for three days, which he did, seeing the Gentlemen v Players match at the Oval, dining with Edgar Bruce and going to the theatre. The six-week course began on 2 July and he clearly did not enjoy it, referring to it as "the usual toil"; "didn't go out until my daily toil was over"; "a very disagreeable day". During the six weeks he developed sciatica and was on the sick list for several days. Miss Morton was also unwell and Mr Parlby "had rather a bad spasm". But Mr Parlby recovered and did some sketching at Bow Arrow

Castle and Chesil Beach while Charles "managed to hobble down to the station" with Mildred and soon came off the sick list. When Mr Parlby and Mildred left he wrote that "I was dreadfully tired" and he also heard "that we are to move to Ireland in September". When the six-week course finally ended on 13 August, he wrote "I can't be too thankful!!!!"

Just before that "there was a wreck on the Chesil Beach, the schooner *Sapphire* from Newcastle to Dublin with coals, not being able to get out of the bay, ran ashore. Her crew were saved by rocket apparatus." There was another wreck at the beginning of the following month "while my darling and I were on the Chesil Beach, the Norwegian barque *Christiane* came ashore.Two men jumped off and were drowned, one after drifting about for about three hours. The rest were saved. A fearful sight." The following day crowds of people came to see the wreck. Roger's few memories of Portland include these two wrecks.

Charles had greater fortune at sea at the end of August when Edgar Bruce came down in Jameson's yacht *Samcena*. Jameson kindly asked Charles to sail with him in the Dorset Yacht Club regatta which he every much enjoyed. "We started at 10.30 and finished the first round (13 miles) soon after one. Then the wind dropped and when we had got about threequarters of the way round, second time, we were becalmed and began drifting. Eventually however we got a little breeze and won the race, after two rounds. No other yacht anywhere near us." After this success he was asked to race again three days later. This was a "splendid race, but we split our Spinnaker in the second round and so were beaten by *Marjorie*." The previous day he had taken Marian and Roger in the Boscowen launch to see the regatta.

At the beginning of September "we paraded for inspection by HRH Prince Edward of Saxe Weimar" who lunched with the regiment. The following day there was a large party "to meet their serene highnesses". Charles and Marian then set off for Wells and Bath. They found Wells "a very nice old place with picturesque gates to the Cathedral Close". The cathedral itself was "small but handsome"; the Vicar's Close "a charming place with little old-fashioned houses and gardens." They attended morning service at the cathedral with a small choir but the "singing not bad" including "one very wheezy old chorister, about 90". Bath Abbey they "liked pretty well".

When they returned to Portland the channel squadron had come into port. They staged a grand "attack" by the blue jackets of the squadron which was "great fun"; a mess dinner to meet the officers of the channel squadron; a cricket match where "being over confident, we were beaten"; dances on board the *Agincourt* and the *Achilles* and dinner with the admiral and a dance on board the *Minotaur* before the fleet set sail for Torbay.

Charles also had to set sail, in his case to Ireland, and therefore decided to move the family to Weymouth, where he found some lodgings "which seemed suitable at 7 Gloucester Terrace". After a few days packing he "took the children's baggage" to Weymouth, with them following on a later train. Charles settled them in and returned to Portland. He then finished packing and clearing before giving over the house at Prospect Place that they had occupied to Mrs Drake the owner "who was not over pleasant". He had to pay £3-9-10 for dilapidations at Prospect Place.

A few days later Marian and Roger went with Charles when he embarked on the *Assistance*. "My darling dined on board with me, though we had some difficulty in getting off. She went ashore in St Clair's gig, I seeing her ashore. Bade "good bye" to her on the quay, for how long we can't tell. May God take care of us while we are parted from one another."

CHAPTER FIVE

CHARLES' FINAL YEARS

It took a day and a half to sail from Portland to Queenstown, after which Charles went with his detachment to Listowel. He wrote that it was "not a bad looking town" but, as the "quarters (where the detachment was housed) were wretched", he stayed in the Listowel Arms "which seems comfortable". He was soon into the Irish way of life, attending the first day of the Listowel Races which was "great fun" with "thousands of people on the course" although the second day there "not so many people" and not "such good sport".

Things were not so good two days later when "I moved from the hotel into my quarters at the workhouse" which he felt was a "wretched place" and "not fit to put anyone into". The Irish weather was equally bad: when he tried to go out for a walk with a fellow officer, they "were driven back by the rain" and they were unable to attend an entertainment that evening for the same reason. There was another example of the Irish way of life on the Sunday when "we went to church" but "owing to the church clock being fast, we were rather late".

After that Charles was soon replaced and was able to leave Ireland being reunited with his family and finding them all well, after an absence of only three weeks. Two days later he "took Roger and Geoffrey to their first school – a kindergarten on the Dorchester Road." At the end of the week they "took baby (Gertrude Alice) to be photographed" but after that "my darling (Marian) had scarcely anything to eat, and was very bad in the evening. Please God she is not going to be ill!" Fortunately she was much better the next day and Charles took Roger and Geoffrey to pick blackberries.

Early in November Charles took Geoffrey and Louis to Yeovil Junction where they were handed over to Mildred to go to Manadon. He then took Roger to London where they went to the zoo and met up with Marian, baby Gertrude Alice and her nurse Mary Merritt who all came by a later train. Gertrude Alice was still referred to as

49

Gertrude by Charles in his diary but came to be known as Alice or by the family as 'girlie' (she will be referred to as Alice from now on). Roger and Alice were taken by Mary to Stanway while Charles and Marian stayed at Berkhamstead and then returned to London where they saw the new Prince's Theatre with Edgar Bruce and went to a number of other productions as well as seeing Willie at the Oxford and Cambridge Club.

When it was time for them to go to Stanway Charles "felt unwell" and had to go down by a later train. He was "very ill" when he got there "and had to send for Mr Worts who relieved me and I had a pretty good night." He had to stay in for the next few days, but by the end of the month they were able to resume their social visits in Colchester calling on "the Morisons (in), Mrs George Round (out) and Mrs Ord (in)". They also heard from Mrs Parlby and Mildred how things were going at Manadon.

At the end of December Charles and Marian took Roger and Alice to Lichfield with Mary Merritt, installed the children and Mary in lodgings and then went to stay at Pool House. Charles went to Bristol to meet Geoffrey and Louis off the train from Manadon and they changed to the *Midland Express* to travel to Lichfield. Early in the New Year 1884 "my darling and I, with the three boys, drove up to Wall and called on the Stokes and saw the church." They also took the three children to see Lichfield Cathedral and then to dine at Pool House.

All this was because Charles and Marian had decided to leave the children at Lichfield while they both went to Ireland. "The hard time of parting came at last, and we left our darlings behind, confident in the care of Mary and the two kind aunts (Emily and Georgiana), who have been so good about them. It was a bitter trial, but it had to be undertaken, and we didn't act without due thought and prayer. God grant all may be well." Mary was clearly in a very trusted position by this time and she was sent a cheque for £8 in January, another for £12-12-6, including her wages, in February and a final settlement of Lichfield bills £8-0-9 with a cheque for Mary for £5 in March.

Charles and Marian sailed for Dublin and then on to Listowel to join his detachment and enter into the Irish way of life. One day the hounds from Tralee came to Balinrudding but they didn't have much sport. Two days later they "went to see a quaint old woman, named Joy, who has lived for 54 years in a sort of drain under the Tralee

Road near the bridge and brought up six children." They then went
to Limerick, staying at the Cruise's Hotel. Charles composed a suitable limerick:

> If you happen to travel near Limerick
> And put up in the Cruise's Hotel
> You'll get nothing done when you're wanting it quick,
> And they don't know the use of a bell.

Charles had to be in Limerick for examinations which were "ridicu-
lously easy" but they could not test his drill as it was wet, and he had
to return to complete it a week later. The Irish weather continued to
be unpredictable and "in another violent hurricane, we drove (with
difficulty, against the wind) to Ballybunion. The scene was
magnificent but we could hardly stand." At the end of the month
"we were asked to a dance at the Hickie's, but it turned out to be a
hoax." They also joined the local church choir and went to choir
practice – "five people including ourselves".

There was plenty of social life for Marian, who Charles now
starts to call Mim in his diary, with a number of service families
stationed over there, such as the Rushbridgers, as well as families
who lived in Ireland. On 11 February "Mim and I (together with two
other ladies) went for a walk through Lord Kenmare's demesne to
Ross Castle, where we had a magnificent view, the hills being covered with snow." Two days later when they called on Mrs Massy
they discovered that the Massys "had been flooded out of their house
last night" and that Captain Massy "had gone to Ennismore". Finding Mrs Massy alone, "we asked her to dine with us, which she did".
But two days later, when Charles shot with Massy, there was "some
little unpleasantness caused by the misinterpretation of a remark of
my darling to Mr Royse, regarding Captain Massy having left Mrs
M all alone and going to Ennismore." This understanding was soon
cleared up as he "went out snipe shooting near Lixnaw with Massy,
but only shot one brace of snipe, and got a fearful ducking." Two
days later they had "a very nice little dinner" at the Massys.

When they first arrived in Listowel the land commissioners were
there but, when they moved on to Killarney, Charles and Marian
"moved into the big room which the Haughton's had". Over the next
week or so Charles did some decorating of the sitting room and they
then held an 'at home'.

However, their future plans now changed again as Charles was "very pleased" on 20 February to receive a "telegram to say that General White had written to offer me the appointment of ADC at Colchester." This was followed by "General White's very kind letter by morning post" the next day. He "replied to it at once, accepting his offer" to rejoin the staff of Eastern District. They left Listowel for Tralee on 26 February where they saw Dick King-Harman and Charles performed in a concert with him. Then it was on to Dublin where they stayed at the Shelbourne Hotel and "met an extraordinary Mr Farrell, who was very proud of showing off his skill as a pianist and singer."

They left Ireland for the last time and landed at Holyhead going on to Beaumaris and Bangor, where they bought a doll for Alice for 6d. 1 March was "the first St David's Day I ever spent in Wales. However we were soon out of the principality" and arrived in Lichfield "so glad to be with our darling children once more" and finding them "all well, barring slight colds". They took Roger and Geoffrey to the cathedral service in the morning. Charles then went on to London for two days where he bought a kilt for Louis for £1-1-6, dined at the club, saw Edgar Bruce and went to the theatre. He then picked up his two dogs, Puck and Tatters, from Euston and went to Stanway to make arrangements to move the family back to Colchester.

Having seen General White, he made enquiries about houses and saw one or two over the next few days before meeting Marian in London to do a lot of shopping. They saw two more houses in Colchester before "finally choosing 7 Beverley Road". But until they could move there, they took lodgings at 21 Crouch Street, which was where they entertained Oscar Wilde. Charles went to the office for the first time on 18 March, the children joining them from Lichfield two days later. The next day was Roger's seventh birthday and they celebrated the three boys' birthdays. Louise and Maude came in with Dr Hill and General White called in with his daughter, but Gerald Parlby missed the train at Harwich and could not come. But a few days later he did come over and "we went with the three boys to see Guinett's Circus which was very good."

Charles was officially "gazetted ADC to General White" on 25 March and, having secured this position, he decided to buy a horse. He lunched with Dr Hill at University Club in London, after which they went to see the horses at Tattersalls. Two days later, on 31

March, he bought a black mare, Kitty, which cost him £35-18-0, bringing her down to Colchester the following day by the 5.38 train. He and Marian then went to a sale at Fullar's where they bought a phaeton – a light four-wheeled open carriage – and by the end of April they were able to go out together with Kitty harnessed to the new carriage for the first time when "she went very well". By then they had moved into their new house in Beverley Road, the rent of the house and stable being £13-4-0 a month. March and April were unusually expensive months, and in addition to the cost of the mare, the purchase of the phaeton and some other things that they bought for the house at the sale came to £27-4-6.

Charles and Marian's lives at Colchester settled into what must have been a familiar pattern. Charles accompanied the general for the Easter Monday battle which took place at Portadown Hill near Portsmouth. When they went over the battleground Charles "was very bad with toothache, and never slept a wink all night" so the following morning he "went first thing to a dentist and had my tooth out – a real bad one." When it came to the battle there was "so great a crowd that no one could well say which side won, but it was generally supposed that the battle was drawn." He returned to Colchester to find that "Geoffrey, Louis and baby have been suffering from a slight attack of chicken pox, but they are nearly well again." He then wrote out the general's report on the manoeuvres.

Working for the general involved attending a number of classes. Charles "triangulated the Abbey Field and discovered that in 19 years I had nearly forgotten all I ever knew about surveying"; he "got a good deal bothered about scales" in topography; and attended classes in military law, tactics and fortification. This eventually led to examinations: "a difficult paper in fortification and a not very hard one in tactics". The next day topography and military law: "neither very hard I think". He also accompanied the general inspecting troops, joining him in Bury St Edmunds to see Lady Bristol present new colours to the third Suffolk Regiment, and going on to Ely where they saw the fourth Suffolk Regiment in the field. Charles took advantage of this occasion to go on to London for a regimental dinner. He also took the opportunity to go to Lord's for two days to see Gentlemen of England v Australians and to see Edgar Bruce and to attend a production.

Socially, there were numerous visits such as having dinner at Mrs George Round's, making afternoon calls such as driving to call on the Hawkins' (out), Ords' (out) and Holroyds (in). Some visits involved the boys such as taking Roger and Geoffrey to Lexden Park and having a walk with Mrs Brock or taking them to church. On one occasion Marian was "at home looking after the children as Mary had gone for a holiday". There were visitors too - Sissie and Arthur Coode came for a few days as did his father. There was also lawn tennis at Stanway – on one occasion Charles played five sets of tennis with Maude and Alice. Charles' brother Edward came to stay at the time of the Queen's Birthday Parade. He had brought his camera and "took some photographs of us". When they went to Stanway, Charles says that Edward "photographed every one and everything", before leaving on an evening train.

Their normal routine was upset on 22 April when "about 9.20 a.m. while we were at breakfast, the whole house was violently shaken. We couldn't make out what had happened but supposed it was an earthquake, which turned out to be the case. It had wrecked many houses in the neighbourhood, overthrown the spire of the congregational church, and done much damage in Colchester. I never before experienced such a sensation and hope I never may again. Thank God, no harm happened to us, and no lives are reported lost, or injuries sustained in the neighbourhood. The whole place was naturally much excited all the day." Roger says in his reminiscences that this was "my most vivid recollection of Colchester".

The following day they were to have dined out at Mr Keeling's "but he wrote to say that his kitchen had sustained such damage from the earthquake that he couldn't give his dinner party." The Jacksons' with whom "we were to have dined at Wyvenhoe Hall, have had their house completely wrecked." The next day he rode out to Peldon and Langenhoe to see the desolation wrought by the earthquake. "I couldn't believe how complete it was." When they went with Roger to Wyvenhoe later to see the damage it was "nothing like as bad as Peldon and Langenhoe", but there was "still much destruction". Roger remembers that old General Orde took several people, "of whom I was one round in his coach-and-four to see the damage". The family attended a crowded service "to thank God for His great mercy in having spared us while He gave us a terrible warning of His presence." Plans were soon afoot for an earthquake concert, although when Charles saw the proof of the concert bill he "had rather a jerk" when he heard that Mrs White (the general's wife) was unable to sing. "The result was that we had to take her name out of the bill." When the concert came off "it was a grand success, many being turned away": they made a profit of £40.

However, life returned to normal. July saw the production of *The Charm* in London, as well as a visit with the general to Yarmouth for a long day which involved "striking and pitching camp twice, as well as some outpost work". August saw garden parties at Lexden Park, Mrs George Round's, Stanway and one given by General White for 200 at the Garrison Cricket Ground as well as a number of lawn tennis parties. In the middle of the month Roger went to stay at Manadon, escorted by Edward, while Geoffrey and Louis stayed in Colchester. Charles and Marian went to Oxford, Cheltenham, Tintern, Monmouth, Raglan, Gloucester, Bath, Reading, Betchworth and then London and back to Colchester.

Charles had to go to Plymouth to attend a funeral in the middle of September, after which he drove out to Manadon "and had a hearty welcome" and "a little walk with dear Mother" (Mrs Parlby). But he had to return quickly and brought Roger back with him to Colchester. In October promotion was on the way and he went to London "and interviewed the Military Secretary about my promotion". He was promoted to the rank of major in 1885.

There was a "pyrotechnic display" in the garden for the children's benefit on 5 November. But an even bigger treat was produced a few days later when the new pony, Toby, who cost £13-3-6, was met at the station. Roger had a ride on Toby the next day, but he was to be more successful than his brothers. Louis and Geoffrey were taken for rides but two weeks later Geoffrey "threw himself off Toby and grazed his face and knee" and the following month "Louis fell off the pony and was a good deal shaken, but fortunately not badly hurt". Roger remembers that "Geoffrey did not take to riding so I practically had the pony to myself. He ran away with me once, but we fetched up safely in the stable-yard." He also remembers that "I had my first day's hunting on Toby, led by Farmfield, my father's soldier-groom."

Charles received "several presents" for his birthday on 16 November and the following night "Dr and Mrs Hill and Maude dined with us to keep my birthday". Two days later they went to "Madame Card's *séance* at the new Corn Exchange, which was most amusing". So much so that the following day Dr Hill and Louise went with him to see Madame Card again. One wonders what she foresaw for Charles for within 13 months he would be dead and his funeral *cortège* would be setting out from his house for his burial at Stanway.

Charles refers to himself as "feeling seedy" on a number of occasions throughout his diaries. In May 1884 he says "I was seedy at night, with the sharp pain I have sometimes". But it was the onset of winter and the number of productions that he was involved in at the end of each year that seems to have put him most at risk. On Boxing Day 1884 "I was very seedy with cold on the chest, but had to sing and recite at an entertainment". The next two days saw him in bed, then feeling better he went into the office, but the following day "had to stay in again, as my cold was very bad".

That winter he recovered and in the only diary of his activities in 1885 – a brief walking tour in March – he managed 132 miles in six days averaging 4.06 miles an hour, writing on the second morning that he was "up in good time and feeling very fit." The tour took him from Chappel, near Colchester, to Lichfield and he had some interesting companions at the different places where he stayed. On the first night he "slept on a sofa in a sitting room" with a party which gave him "a curious experience of the ways of horse dealers and being pitched into the middle of a party playing nap". The next night his "only companion was a middle-aged clergyman, with whom I had a great deal of conversation". And two nights later "my sole companion in the small room where I fed, was a perfectly deaf inspector of schools, named Collins, who would insist on conversation, and was rather a nuisance in consequence." The final night he stayed at "a very indifferent hotel" where he "partook of greasy chops in a greasy commercial room in company with two young bagmen of a very inferior description."

The last three diary entries – also from March 1885 – show Charles continuing to live his life in a familiar way: walking to Wall from Lichfield and calling on the Stokes; travelling to London, dining there and going to the theatre; and seeing Willie at the Oxford and Cambridge Club and attending another production.

The circumstances of his sudden death are known from Roger's reminiscences and from press reports. Roger says that he "neglected a cold caught at Christmas 1885" and insisted on going and taking part in "an entertainment at which he had promised to sing". The press report of his death says that on 30 December he went out "but subsequently feeling unwell and a little asthmatical, he was attended by Dr Churchill and afterwards by Dr Lane (military doctors) but nothing serious was apprehended until Monday morning (4 January), when the symptoms became so alarming that Dr Veale, physician to the Essex and Colchester Hospital, was called in, and various members of his family were telegraphed for." The following day a short will was drawn up, signed by Charles with his brother Willie and Richard Hill acting as witnesses, leaving everything to Marian. But Charles "never rallied and though conscious up to within a short period of his death, he rapidly succumbed to the disease." The cause of his death was "inflammation of the lungs which developed very rapidly". "We understand that Dr Hill and family were in attendance upon the deceased up to the last; that his father, his brother (Willie) and his sister (Sissie) arrived yesterday, but he had lost consciousness before his father arrived at his bedside."

The press report points out that "it was a singular coincidence that his death took place at ten minutes before noon on the last day of his occupancy of the post of *Aide-de-Camp* to General White, he having recently been appointed to the adjutancy of the first battalion of the Queen's Royal West Surrey Volunteers at Croydon, to take up his appointment for five years, he and his family had proposed to leave Colchester for Croydon at the close of the present month."

Roger had "a vivid recollection of his funeral procession, the gun carriage, the escort, and great numbers of soldiers of all arms, who voluntarily – for he was immensely popular with the garrison – marched the four miles, in deep snow to Stanway, where he was buried." When one reads the account of the scale of the funeral in the Essex Standard this is not surprising. The *cortège* started out from their house in Beverley Road: "the weather was intensely cold, and the state of the roads extremely slippery". Large numbers of people braved the elements and the sight of a funeral with full military honours was a very imposing one. "The blinds were drawn at all the private houses in the neighbourhood, while in the town many of the tradespeople and other residents showed their respect by putting up shutters or drawing blinds during the funeral. The flag of the Colchester Conservative Association and the Working Men's Club was half-mast high."

The coffin "was placed on a gun carriage provided for the purpose, the order was given to 'present arms' which was done with great smartness, the bayonets glittering in the sun which was then shining, while the officers and others who were gathered around raised their helmets. The coffin was then covered with a Union Jack, and the deceased's hat, accoutrements etc. were placed on top, also a number of wreaths and other floral offerings sent by loving friends."

The wreaths included a cross sent by General White, a cross from Edgar Bruce, Prince's Theatre, London "with deepest sympathy" and a wreath from Mr and Mrs Hole "with much love and sincere remembrances". Others who sent wreaths or crosses included Major King-Harman, Revd John Parlby, Mrs Parlby and Miss Parlby (Mildred) and Mr and Mrs Arthur Coode.

The procession set off with a firing party of 200 men, the band of the Bedfordshire Regiment playing a funeral march, then the body borne on the gun carriage drawn by six black horses and among those walking on either side General White, then the deceased's charger led by two soldiers and draped in black cloth, with the boot and spur hanging reversed in the stirrup at either side, and then the chief mourners – first carriage, Willie and Edward – his brothers; second carriage – Arthur Coode (Sissie's husband), William Hole (Emily Parlby's husband), and Reginald and Walter Parlby; third carriage (Dr Hill's carriage) three female servants (including Mary).

There was a large attendance at Stanway church including General Radcliffe and Mr Jas Round MP. "The coffin was carried into the church where in 1881, the deceased gallant officer was married to the rector's daughter." After the service the body was "borne to the grave which had been prepared on the south side of the west end and was neatly lined with moss and decorated with white chrysanthemums and lilies, a cross of white chrysanthemums being placed at the head." The mourners then gathered around the grave, the band was stationed nearby and the firing party were placed in line. "At this point the scene was a most touching one and there were not a few of the spectators as well as the deceased's relatives, who were moved to tears." On the conclusion of the Burial Service, the firing party of 200 fired three volleys each, each volley being followed by the customary roll of muffled drums, and the ceremony ended. "The mourners then took a last look at the coffin, containing him whom they so fondly loved." Charles was only 38 years old and Marian now had to bring up the four children on an estate which was valued at £393-14-1.

PART TWO
ROGER AND GEOFFREY MOTT

Roger Mott   Geoffrey Mott

CHAPTER SIX

MANADON AND OXFORD

Roger, Geoffrey and Louis often stayed at Manadon and Roger comments that "my love of the place must have been generated in me from my earliest days" when he spent two years there while his parents, Charles and Gertrude, were in India. Visits to Manadon continued after Gertrude's death. When Charles and Marian had to move from Colchester in April 1882, Charles left Colchester with the children by the 9.20 train. "Roger and I went by underground, the rest by cab to Paddington, and I saw them off by the 11.45 train" to Manadon. The children were looked after there for a fortnight and, when Charles and Marian joined them, Charles wrote "so glad to be with our darling children once more". At the beginning of May "I walked into Plymouth. My darling drove in with the children and Mildred and the chicks had their photographs taken". They all stayed at Manadon until 8 May when Charles and Marian went to stay with his sister Sissie and her husband Arthur, the children remaining at Manadon. A week later they picked Roger up at Mutley station going on to stay with the Holes at Parke, Bovey Tracey before the family settled in at Dawlish. When the photographs of the children arrived, they were sent to Mrs Parlby, Marion and Emily Parlby, aunts Emily and Georgiana Mott and Sissie Coode.

When Charles and Marian had to move again at the beginning of 1883, Charles left Portland with the three boys. "I saw Mrs Clarke and the boys off from Yeovil Junction for Plymouth." The following day he "heard of the boys' safe arrival at Manadon. Very thankful". It was not until the middle of March that he was able to meet the three boys at Yeovil Junction "who had come up from Manadon with Reggie (Parlby), and took them back with us".

In November "I left Weymouth with Geoffrey and Louis by the 12 noon train for Yeovil Junction, where I handed them over to Mildred to take charge of them to Manadon." Roger remained behind on this occasion and went with his father to London, visiting the zoo before he went off to Stanway with his sister Alice under the charge of Mary. At the end of the year Charles and Marian with Roger, Alice and Mary went by train to Lichfield. The following day Charles took the train to Bristol where he met Geoffrey and Louis off the *Flying Dutchman* from Manadon from where they travelled to Lichfield.

On 11 August 1884 it was Roger's turn to go to Manadon on his own. "Dr Hill escorted R to Waterloo, whence Edward took him to Manadon." Charles arrived at Manadon on 20 September where he "had a hearty welcome" and two days later he took Roger back by train reaching "Waterloo about six. Roger and I had some dinner at Liverpool Street and went down by *Continental Express*" to Colchester.

Roger paints a fascinating picture of the time he and his brothers spent at Manadon and of the role that the house and its occupants played in shaping their lives and in giving them security, with both their parents dying young. I have quoted him at length:

"As the years went by, we used to make annual visits to the grandparents, and Manadon was like a second home to us. There was always the thrill of travelling by the *Flying Dutchman* - a precursor of the *Cornish Riviera Express* - Geoffrey was always sick in the train in those days! There was the grim excitement of the box Tunnel, where my father would say 'In we go Robinson. . . Out we come, Jones'. There was the arrival at Mutley station, where the Manadon carriage-and-pair and the luggage-cart met us. There was the joy of waking up next morning and realizing that we were at Manadon again.

Often, we would be out and about before breakfast, renewing acquaintance with our favourite haunts. Nursery breakfast was at nine, family prayers at half-past, and the family meal at ten; we would look on at that, and were always given fruit at the finish. Later, we would accompany aunt Millie on her housekeeping business. The best part of which, to us, was the visit to the storeroom, which meant small treats in the shape of prunes, preserved fruit or angelica!

There was never any difficulty amusing ourselves. The gardens and grounds were extensive and we made our own amusements. The chief of these was 'running trains'. On high ground to the west of the house stood 'The Belvedere', a circular building with a fire-place and furnished with table and chairs. This was 'Paddington'. A path from this ran through the rookery, past some greenhouses, and down to the house; from here, another path led to the stables, and on past a huge Macracarpa - my mother's tree, planted when she was born. (A tree was planted on the arrival of every child and grand-child). Here was a junction, one path leading to the potting sheds and walled-garden entrance, the other outside the walls, past the ladies' garden - a little enclosed space with areas allotted to each of the daughters of the house - and on to the back drive leading to Knackersknowle, later known as Crown Hill, a mere village in those days, before the barracks were built. At intervals along these paths were seats, and we gave each the name of a station between Paddington and Plymouth - Reading, Didcot, Swindon, Bath and so on.

Another amusement was to run down the main drive to the lodge, against time, and sometimes we would push the old three-wheeled pram for that journey; it got away once, down the hill from the house, and overturned at the first gate, but the occupant took no harm.

There was a pony for us to ride, the old grey 'Silvertail', he attained the great age of 36. As we got older we were taught to shoot, the weapon being a pin-fire gun, and stalking rabbits was grand fun. Then there was archery; targets were set up in front of the house and when we were older we were allowed to shoot on the Devon and Cornwall archery ground, which was on the property, and abutted on the Devonport road. This boasted a timber-built thatched clubhouse in which dinners and dances were held from time to time; the big room was hung with shields, bearing the coats-of-arms of the various presidents and ladies paramount of the society, whose annual meeting was a great and picturesque event in the life of Manadon.

We would frequently fish or boat in one of the two ponds below the house. I fell in one Sunday on the way back from church, but aunt Millie hauled me out by the slack of my breeches. The other aquatic amusement was sailing boats. My grandfather was a keen yachtsman, a member of the Royal Western Yacht Club. He gave me a beautiful model yacht, and taught me how to sail it on the pond. Alternatively we would race little boats along the Devonport leat. There were two leats running through the property, the other being the Plymouth leat, constructed by order of Sir Francis Drake. We used to organize bumping-races on the Devonport leat - a good mile of it - and it kept us happy for hours on end, until summoned to lunch by a big bell rung at the house.

Occasionally, we would run paperchases over the estate. I remember one which finished up with a gorgeous cream-tea at 'Pounds', a neighbouring property belonging to the Chappell-Hodge's - known by the nickname of the 'Apple Stodges'! Another paperchase finished at Ham, the home of a dear old early Victorian lady, Miss Trelawney Collins.

Then, there were drives, for carriages of all sorts were kept at Manadon in those days. Plymouth was one of the objectives, and Gaylard's toy-shop the mecca of that place for us. There we bought little boats, and other things, with the tips that kind grandparents, aunts or uncles had supplied. My eldest uncle, Gerald, a lieut-colonel, Royal Horse Artillery, was an excellent whip, and used to drive the regimental coach; on one occasion he had it at Manadon, and I remember him taking a large party to a meet of the Dartmoor Otter Hounds at Puslinch bridge on the river Yealm.

The hounds took a red-hot drag up the Silveridge leat, but after a time we boys were hauled back, to our great disgust, before the pack came up to their otter, for it was thought we were getting too far from our lunch. On another occasion, uncle Gerald took us with him in his tandem. Halfway down the drive he found that his man had forgotten his sword, so sent him back for it, telling him to meet us at the end of the back drive. The foolish man came by the front drive, which meant that we had to wait for him. Uncle Gerald was furious, and being late he drove like Jehu the rest of the day, which included a hectic drive down the steep lane to Plymbridge. The cart rocked, but uncle Gerald was a fine driver, and we arrived safely at the foot of the hill.

We learned to play tennis, and there was an occasional boys' cricket match; we also went fly-fishing, at which Geoffrey was the only one to show any skill. The uncles used to shoot, either round Manadon, or at their father's property at Sampford Spiney; I went with them now and again, but found I was a very poor shot.

In wet weather there was always something to do in the house. My earliest recollection was a day when aunt Millie turned out all the drawers in the ivory cabinet in the drawing room. Many years later I bought that cabinet -which I had always admired- and found that it was made at Vizagapatam in about 1750, and is a rare piece.

Manadon was a capital house in which to play hide-and-seek. Let me try to describe it. A granite portico led to the square front-hall, out of which double doors led to the dining room and drawing room. Another door led to the inner hall, with passages leading to the library, which could also be approached through the drawing room, and to the breakfast room at the other end of the house - from this room there were steps, leading down to the extensive cellars. The main staircase, wide and made of black oak, went up from the inner hall. From near the breakfast room a wide stone passage led to the pantry, and on to the large kitchen, scullery and servants' hall. At the back of the house was a courtyard, with a magnificent hydrangea bush, and containing the dairies and other outbuildings.

The main staircase led to a wide passage on the first floor. Here was my grandmother's room, with a powdering-cupboard which contained an array of medicine-bottles, one containing Gregory powder - of unpleasant memory! The other rooms on the first floor were the 'Red room' and the 'Chintz room', each with a fine granite fireplace and its own dressing room. A short flight of steps led to the oldest part of the house, over the breakfast room and pantry, and containing three bedrooms, with three more over them; these were my grandfather's bed and dressing rooms, and bachelor quarters. On the top floor were the day and night nurseries, and various bedrooms originally devoted to the daughters of the house. At the back of the house were the housekeeper's room, those of various menservants and maidservants and the laundry. There was no bathroom in the house when we were children, and only one WC, which was sacred to the ladies. The men folk had to go to various premises outside, concealed by shrubberies!

No smoking was allowed in the house; anyone wishing to indulge in that (to my grandfather) pernicious habit had to go to the 'arch-room', over the stables, or to the servants' hall, after the occupants had gone to bed!

An archway, between the stables and the harness and saddle rooms, led to a courtyard containing two coach houses, and beyond was a range of farm buildings and a couple of cottages.

I wonder how many servants there were at Manadon in those days? Indoor and outdoor, what good friends they all were!

Those were days of family prayers; they were held in the mornings in the breakfast room, and on Sunday nights in the dining room. When the family and guests were assembled, the staff trooped in, led by the housekeeper, then the maids, and the footman and butler whipped in. The cook was excused in the mornings, as she had to be busy with breakfast.

Church parade on Sunday mornings brought one or more carriages to the door for the grandparents and the elder ladies; the young and energetic walked across a few fields to Pennycross church. The family pew was in the chancel, and the staff had a couple of pews in the body of the church, where they were under their master's eye. The horses having been stabled in adjoining farm buildings, the fat coachman, in all the splendour of livery, stumped up the aisle to his place - and then (it always seemed) the service could begin! My grandfather always read the lessons - and he did it beautifully - but, though in Holy Orders, he never took any other part in the service.

There were often cousins staying in the house at the times we were there Arbuthnott's or Thurlow's, and there seemed always to be visitors as well. On one occasion, uncle Walter, who was then up at Oxford, brought several of his friends from St John's College for an archery meeting. They were a jolly crowd, always ragging; the arch room was put at their disposal, and there they could make as much row as they liked - and they did!

A visit to Manadon usually meant other visits - to my uncle and aunt, Arthur and Sissie Coode at Trevarthian, St Austell, and to Parke, Bovey Tracey where uncle William Hole and aunt Emily reigned, with their only child, Willie, known as the 'Buttonhole'! Parke was great fun, and there were always ponies to ride there."

What comes through so strongly from these memories is how much they enjoyed their visits to Manadon and the stability that it gave to their lives. His younger brother Geoffrey had equally fond memories: "many of our holidays were spent with our grandparents and these formed some of the happiest days of my life."

Although many of their holidays were spent happily at Manadon, there was the important issue of their education to resolve. While in Colchester Roger remembers that he went to a little day school where he began learning Latin. But soon after their father's funeral, the children moved with Marian from Colchester to Oxford and 2 Winchester Road so that they could go to school at the Oxford Preparatory School, now known as the Dragon School. Her father, Dr Hill, had been headmaster of Magdalen College School, and his knowledge of Oxford and education would have been very helpful to her in making this decision.

At the beginning of the summer term, Roger and Geoffrey started at the Oxford Preparatory School. Roger remembers that there were about 60 boys there and that the headmaster was the Reverend A.E. Clarke. But "tragedy befell the school in our second term and I well remember when C.C. Lynam ('The Skipper') came into school, with tears running down his cheeks, and told us that Mr Clarke was dead."

'The Skipper' now became headmaster "what a happy man he was, and immensely popular with the boys; a grand organizer, an artist and above all a seaman. He used to sail on the Upper Thames and won many races."

Like his father, Roger enjoyed acting and he played some important parts in the annual Shakespeare productions, instituted by 'The Skipper' who was also stage manager and painted all the scenery. The first production was *Macbeth* in which Roger played Macduff. The following year he played Laertes in *Hamlet* and he was even called upon soon after he had left to play Portia in *The Merchant of Venice*.

He also played for the first XV Rugby and first X1 Cricket teams and discovered that he had an aptitude for cross-country running when some of the paperchases were run. Geoffrey discovered he had the same ability, but in rather different circumstances. "Playing cricket one day, I in some way managed to offend the master in charge. He, being a somewhat stern individual and renowned for being not sparing of the rod, I refused to go up to him when called. Instead, in a panic, I set off across country as fast as my legs would carry me, pursued, by his order, by all the boys on the field. Somehow I managed to outdistance them, and reached home before dark. Next morning in fear and trepidation, I entered his classroom, but, to my amazement and infinite relief, he said 'Mott, I am not going to punish you as you ran so well'."

Academically, Roger did much better than Geoffrey. He reports that "I was the first Dragon on the Eton roll, but did not go there, as I had also won a scholarship and an exhibition at Wellington College, and this enabled Geoffrey to be sent to Marlborough, which my mother could not otherwise have afforded for him." Geoffrey says that he had shown little aptitude for work, but he had been despatched to various other schools in the hope that he would win a scholarship. He achieved a near miss at Malvern but the consolation prize that he was offered was insufficient and so he was sent to Marlborough. The same problem of lack of money meant that Louis was sent to the United Services College at Westward Ho, which had been created in 1874 for service officers and where, for a minimum fee, they received an adequate education in Spartan conditions. Rudyard Kipling had attended the school a few years earlier and his *Stalky & Co* drew on his experiences there. But Louis coped well, played in the first XI Hockey team, and succeeded in securing a place at Keble College, Oxford.

During their time in Oxford the three brothers used to attend church every Sunday morning and "in the afternoons would go either to the cathedral or to Magdalen or New College Chapels, which gave us a love of good church-music and singing." They were able to do this through the Hill family's connections with the president of Magdalen who had married one of Marian's bridesmaids. The Warden of New College, the famous Dr Spooner, was another old friend of the Hill family.

The family kept a boat on the Cherwell and it was in that river that the children learnt to swim – Roger "with great difficulty". They also enjoyed skating on the Cherwell, on the Isis at Iffley Meadows or on the pond at Worcester College. "In the Christmas holidays, there were plenty of children's dances and lots of nice partners." The best dances were given by the Harcourts in their house beyond Magdalen Bridge, but Geoffrey enjoyed dances immensely at the Daniels and Gamlens on consecutive evenings in 1894.

When they were living there, the town of Oxford ended at St Margaret's Road. Summertown was a separate village and Cowley, where Morris later developed his factory, was in the country. "In our days Morris had a small bicycle shop in the town and we used to deal there."

Roger and Geoffrey's achievements at Wellington College and Marlborough were both affected by their initial form placements. Roger started in the middle fifth. "This was a pity because practically all the form consisted of boys of 17 or so, none of whom went any higher, and their attitude to work was not such as to encourage a youngster like myself to work hard. Accordingly I spent a lazy year in that form, and even got beaten for not doing a good exam – it didn't hurt."

Geoffrey says that "I made a great error at the outset". New boys had to sit an examination to determine their form placing and he "went for it, foolishly, as if for a scholarship, the result being that I found myself installed in Shell A, a form in those days below the lower fifth. This seemed to impress my classmates, for they swarmed around me, all eager for help with their prep! Alas I found myself in far too high a form." The result was that his weekly place was bottom of the class and a weekly caning from his housemaster.

Things improved for Roger when he reached the upper fifth and then the lower sixth under E.A. Upcott who read poetry beautifully. He was taught French by Louis Sers who "would roll and smoke cigarettes, and occasionally go to his piano and play and sing charming little French songs or yarn about his old home on Reunion Island."

Geoffrey excelled at Greek irregular verbs but "had no taste whatsoever" for Euclid. He received a "bi-weekly basting" at the hands of the maths master with either racquet handle or a fives bat. "It hurt quite a bit so, for a week or so, I slogged quite hard but to no purpose. After that I stubbornly declined to open the book again, and took my punishment like a lamb."

Roger says that he "was only second-best at most things" except long-distance running where he went in for all the paperchases and "won a 'Bigside' run by a short head which led to my eventually becoming Master of the Hunt." He also enjoyed singing and acting, like his father. He was in the choir throughout his time in the school "going from treble to alto and then baritone". He continued with his acting, twice performing in extracts from plays on Speech Days "once in the presence of King Edward VII, then Prince of Wales".

Two unusual occurrences were a ten week frost one winter when E.C. Upcott, who was a good figure skater, organized skating on the bathing lake. "I was one of the team and passed the third class test for the NSA, and was on the point of examining for the second class when the ice broke up." The other was an outbreak of diptheria which necessitated the school being moved to Malvern for a term while Wellington was being redrained. Unfortunately "a nice boy in my form died of it".

Roger became a school prefect and passed directly into Sandhurst, but Geoffrey's path was much less smooth. He says that he achieved so little success at Marlborough that in 1894 "lest I should be super-annuated, my stepmother took me away" at the end of the Lent term.

The previous month their grandmother, Mrs Emma Parlby, had died and Geoffrey had "a sad letter from aunt Millie about poor grandmama's death". He went to Manadon from Marlborough for the funeral "which went off very well". When Geoffrey had his birthday two weeks later he received a watch from aunt Millie. But in May Gerald Parlby died, soon after getting married, and in the autumn of 1885 their favourite aunt Millie also died and was buried at Pennycross.

Following his removal from Marlborough, Geoffrey's education took an unusual turn. He was sent to a parson in Monmouthshire, Mr Evans, for a year where he was set to work in a Canadian log hut in the garden. For most of the time he was on his own because the only other pupil "got the sack for over-indulgence with one of the maids". Geoffrey did not find the work over-strenuous to say the least and lived a wonderful life in which he was able to indulge his interests in the countryside, especially in hunting, which proved the highlight of the year, and fishing. Within a few days of arriving he went to Pontypool with Mr Evans and bought a fishing licence, flies and a landing net and this showed his tutor's sense of priorities. A few days later they saw a nightingale's nest with four eggs, found a ground wren's nest with five eggs and caught a trout. He continued to fish regularly in the local brook and when he saw the miller at the local mill, he gave him cider which was 'very good'. He went otter hunting on a few occasions on the River Usk once walking about 26 miles in a day. He also went foxhunting at least once a week in the winter.

During the year he spent two weeks with a friend of Mr Evans, Dr James, then headmaster of Cheltenham College. One day when asked what he would like to do he "replied that I would enjoy seeing how many orchids I could find in a day." He arranged for the keenest botanist in the school to have a day off which resulted in them finding no less than eight varieties of wild orchid including the 'Bee' and drinking water out of 'Seven Springs' the source of the Thames. This unusual love of wild flowers for a child is evident in his diary and in his final term at Marlborough he records that he had found *viola odorata*, *helleborus viridis*, *drabaverna* and grape hyacinth *muscari* which he commented was "very rare".

But all this freedom was too good to last and "when I discovered that my tutor was all too fond of the bottle, I realized I was learning literally nothing." The only reference in his diary of 1894 of work with his tutor was in November when Geoffrey wrote that Mr Evans was "jolly sick about something. After doing ten chapters of Livy (unprepared) (Mr Evans) talks about (Geoffrey) being 'slovenly' as he (Mr Evans) slunk out of the room." Eventually Geoffrey "reluctantly confided in my parent, who in 1895 arranged for me to go to Kelly College in Devon."

But Geoffrey, having had a year of freedom and now aged 17, proved to be much too unorthodox in his methods to settle down to school routine and, with a weak headmaster, he admits that his end of term reports were "most disappointing" and his behaviour "disgraceful". After morning school on a Saturday, he would miss lunch, head off for the nearest pack of hounds, run with them and return just in time to line up for the school rugby match. On another occasion, when he was told to stay in the house library after an overnight stomach upset, he broke out of the school grounds and went to a meet of the Otter Hounds eight miles away. At the end of the day's hunting he was introduced to whisky by those present who drew up a 'round robin' asking that he should not be flogged on his return to school. It had no effect, he was caned and 'gated' for the rest of term.

After four terms at Kelly, Geoffrey spent three months at a cramming establishment on the outskirts of Torquay where the teaching "was so full of interest that at the end of a brief spell, I was considered fit to sit for the Sandhurst exam." But he failed one subject and was too old to compete again.

So Roger went to Sandhurst, while Geoffrey had to spend two years cramming for the Regular Army.

CHAPTER SEVEN

EARLY DAYS IN THE ARMY AND THE BOER WAR

Roger entered Sandhurst in September 1895 which he found "great fun". He enjoyed topography but administration and law "bored me stiff" and he "passed out lower than I had passed in". He says that he only played for the 'A' teams at cricket and football but that he did have "the glory of breaking C.B. Fry's leg stump in two after he had made 84!"

Having passed out he joined his father's regiment, the Second Queen's Regiment[31], where his father's former subaltern was now colonel. He was posted to B company which "had no less than three rugby internationals in the battalion", one of whom, R.O.H. Livesay, was also a first-class cricketer and played for Kent. While they were stationed at Woking he had a couple of hunters of his own and "a smart rubber-tyred dog-cart, in which I took a party to and from Ascot each day for the races". He also went with fellow officers to Sandown, Kempton and Windsor, all of which gave him a love for racing. At Aldershot on a transport course "having had some previous driving experience and having succeeded in driving a pair better than others in the class, I was allowed to drive eight miles in a buck-wagon, which had recently arrived for experiment. Accompanied by a corporal with a long whip, I had some splendid drives until, bowling along on the Bagshot road, one of the two centre-pairs came down, and that ended my amusement."

Roger was also fleet of foot and whipped in to the Aldershot Beagles, priding himself on his running. When the battalion carried out a 20-mile march on the final day of manoeuvres on Salisbury Plain in 1898, it proved "almost too much for the youngsters. Determined that none should fall out I began carrying the rifles of these men, and finished up at Ludgershall station with nine across my shoulders, but no man in the company fell out!"

---

[31] The Queen's Royal Regiment was reorganized as the Queen's (Royal West Surrey) Regiment in 1881.

Another highlight of these early years was Queen Victoria's Diamond Jubilee, which proved a very tiring day for the officers involved who were wearing *Levée* dress – gold lace and strapped overalls. Roger remembers that "the procession took some hours to pass and occasionally halted, when we experienced the optical illusion that the houses opposite were moving in the reverse direction to the procession – which had the result that several men fainted." But it was a memorable day and the only one where Roger saw Queen Victoria.

Geoffrey's first introduction to military life was rather different. In the spring of 1897, after only two months of preliminary training, he was posted to the South Wales Borderers at Welshpool. The month of training which followed gave him an introduction to the realities of military life. "The old hands turned up. Many of them were ragged and ill-dressed and I remember the embarrassment I felt, as a very junior subaltern having to march a party of the men into camp in Powys Castle Park swaying from one side of the road to the other!" Fortunately, the colonel was enlightened enough to give them 24 hours to "work it off" after which they had to "toe the line". By the end of the month they had become a good unit.

While serving with the unit, Geoffrey spent two years at Plymouth 'cramming' for the Regular Army. On Sundays a group would drive out to the 'Saracen's Head' at Two Bridges where the host, "a man of exceptional humour", had excellent meats and "an extremely choice cellar!" "Before setting out on the homeward journey we made our crammer brew a large bowl of punch." Geoffrey did not over work until the examination was looming when he surprised his tutor by suggesting that he should stay behind to work over the Christmas vacation, but only on condition that he should hunt two days a week during the vacation, and that, when the others returned, he should have Saturdays off. But, when the day of the exam came close and Geoffrey claimed his Saturday off, he was told that he would get the sack if he went hunting. He ignored the warning, went hunting and was told to leave, but he did not go quietly, arranging for his cab to arrive in the middle of lunch so that he could go round the table, shake hands with instructors and pupils, but pointedly not his own tutor.

He spent the final week before the exams at a crammer near Abingdon where, being determined to pass, he worked hard, was given his commission and joined the South Lancashire Regiment in May 1899.

Two months later the Reverend John Hall Parlby of Manadon died at Parke, Bovey Tracey at the age of 94, removing another strong influence in the upbringing of Roger, Geoffrey and Louis, and all three of them were among the mourners. He was buried in the family vault at a service attended by his children and their husbands or wives and his grandchildren - Emily and William Hole and their son William, Marion and Charles Arbuthnott and their four children, Winifred and Hugh Thurloe and their son Guy, and Reginald Parlby, who, as the eldest surviving son, was now the heir to the estate.

Shortly afterwards both Roger and Geoffrey sailed for South Africa with their regiments to fight the Boers. The SS *Yorkshire*, carrying the second battalion of the Queen's was the first ship to leave England at the end of October, taking them from Southampton to Cape Town. Roger wrote to his stepmother that "two boats came alongside and we heard the following news – Mafeking and Ladysmith have been cut off and invested by the Boers." Then they sailed on to Durban and went by train to Pietermaritzberg, before going on to Escourt, where they arrived by 19 November. Geoffrey left Liverpool at the end of November, taking the same route to Durban, via Cape Town and then on by train to Escourt, where he arrived on Christmas Eve.

Roger found his organizing abilities recognised by being put in charge of transport at Pietermaritzberg where he discovered that "the authorities were in a fearful muddle and kept on changing their orders as to what we should have." He was told that he could get a horse from the Remount depot, but "as the horses had not arrived from Durban ... I bought one to make sure for £30, including saddlery. He was cheap, for prices here are exorbitant." Roger was handed over 32 mules and four ammunition carts, which he took to Escourt by train. "There was some thought that we might be attacked on the last part of the journey, but that did not happen." In Escourt he drew 96 oxen and six wagons, but found that "this place is in as much of a muddle as the last; in fact the whole war seems to have been bungled so far!" But at this stage he was still optimistic about the outcome, writing that "I expect we shall fight a big battle this week and perhaps be in Ladysmith next Sunday."

He first saw action when he went out on a big reconnaissance party. "A scout came galloping in – 'Boers in force half a mile away!' Everyone rushed as hard as they could go and got into a defensive position on the nearest hill. I was sent galloping off for the guns over the most awful country, full of boulders. When I got to the guns, they found they could not get up the hill. Next I was ordered to superintend the loading of as much baggage as possible and get it on the road for home. The Boers were about 2,000 strong and on a commanding hill, about 2,000 yards away; so we determined to retire under cover of night. I packed all I could on to the wagons, made the stationmaster give me an engine and truck for the remainder; packed it up and sent it to Escourt. Once when I was near the artillery, about ten rifle shots were fired at us, but they all fell short; still I was actually 'under fire'." He comments that "we were really lucky in escaping as we were surrounded in a bad position by about 4,000 Boers."

By now General Sir Redvers Buller commanded the British forces, with Brigadier Hildyard commanding the third division which included the Queen's. Roger's assessment of strengths and weaknesses, written in a letter at the end of November, was that "we have no maps here"; that "our mounted infantry are splendid fellows – very daring and good fighters. The infantry are much too slow for the Boers, who are all mounted. Our guns are more accurate, but theirs shoot farther."

On 15 December 1899 during the Battle of Colenso "the moment the infantry advanced *whiz-z-z-pom* came the shells, right among us ... a big one pitched within ten yards of me, but fortunately did not burst! I have got the shell and shall try and bring it home! It was from a 4.7 gun and weighs 32 pounds ... Pilleau took a photograph of me with it." In the battle "our fellows advanced to within 1,200 yards of the enemy, being rained on by shells and bullets all the time. A few got another 200 yards into the village of Colenso, but further than that it was impossible to go, on account of the river." Overall Roger wrote that "a lot of bad, elementary mistakes were made".

He also commented later that "one of Buller's troubles was that he had no proper map of the country – only a blueprint which showed boundaries but no features; so a mounted reconnaissance was ordered, and I was detailed to sketch part of the Tugela river." Geoffrey crossed that same Tugela river in the middle of January 1900 when both Roger's and Geoffrey's regiments were involved in a six-day attack attempting to break through the Boer defences. Roger says that when they took a steep hill on the right, called Spion Kop, "they lost terribly and the worst of it was, when they got there, they found the cross fire so hot as to render the place untenable." During the six days of fighting Geoffrey remembers that he "was within a few yards of a group of generals who were having a conference on Three Tree Hill. They made no attempt to conceal themselves, and were evidently spotted for presently a spray of shrapnel swished over their heads, on which General Clery drew his sword and waved it furiously in the air shouting 'curse the b....s'." Shortly afterwards a Boer shell landed in a farmyard which caused a family of young pigs to dash across in front of the Connaught Rangers. "This was too much for the startled Irishmen, who chivvied them with fixed bayonets!" Another observer of the battle was Winston Churchill, who was acting as a war-correspondent, and Roger remembers "having a chat with him during the battle".

When the withdrawal from Spion Kop was ordered, Geoffrey "had a particularly trying time. Shortly before moving off, my legs began to feel queer, and before long I lost all feeling in them. It was a most alarming experience on that dark drizzly night and I dreaded the idea of being taken prisoner" especially in the light of reports of Boer treatment of prisoners then in circulation. He had to be left behind. Fortunately a stretcher arrived but he had to spend seven hours on it "in sheer agony, the pain becoming increasingly acute". The following day he was borne in scorching sun to the field hospital, but by the time he arrived he was free from pain, which he could only attribute to the effects of the tropical sun.

However, he could not be admitted to hospital, which was too overcrowded, and had to make his way to the director of transport for his regiment who was over two miles away. By the time he got there he collapsed at the director's feet and was immediately sent back to hospital where he learnt by a stroke of luck that his brother Roger was close at hand in charge of his company's transport. The two brothers shared a tent for three days and then rode together to Mount Alice where they watched troops advancing to the attack. Geoffrey observed the Battle of Vaal Krantz "in almost complete security, for the shells of the Boer guns mostly fell harmlessly short of us." Roger remembers the shelling by *pom-pom* of the battalion lying down in close column in a dip of the ground. "Someone counted 80 shells in an hour, but we only had four casualties."

In February the Queen's captured Monte Christo, occupied Colenso and secured a bridgehead across the Tugela River. Roger wrote that "a piece of shell narrowly missed me and my pony". There were several days of heavy fighting in which "our men are having a very trying time; I have to be on the go half the night, taking rations up to them: cannot go in the daytime as our oxen would be too good a target. But tracks are difficult to find in the dark, and the regiment keeps changing position and the sniping is too close to be pleasant." He ended his letter of 25 February "I hope I shall soon be able to write more cheerfully and tell you of the relief of Ladysmith". He *was*, as at the end of the month "our entry into Ladysmith was an occasion to remember; our fellows in rags, but as fit as fleas, and the garrison in spotless clean clothes, but pale and weak." It was Roger who had to fit them out with new clothes, as the quartermaster was taken sick and was sent back to England, so he took over his job as well as continuing his own of transport officer – "but with no extra pay!"

Geoffrey had rejoined his regiment but was sent to hospital where General Clery was in the same ward suffering from phlebitis along with "an unfortunate quartermaster in the next bed to mine who had his foot gnawed by rats one night." Geoffrey was then granted sick leave and opted to accept the hospitality of a colonial, Mrs Landale from Howick, where he was able to recover and indulge in some fishing, although near one pool he found a puff adder curled up which he despatched with a pistol lent to him by his hostess. He even put together a pack of local dogs to look for an otter, which had been seen recently, but they only found a hare and a water buck.

Both regiments were around Ladysmith for a few weeks in March and April and the two brothers were within easy reach of each other. Geoffrey often joined his brother for rides on a horse which Roger provided for him and they had meals together in their respective messes. Roger wrote "we have a jolly little 'officers' *laager*' under a fine acacia tree, and are going to put up a marquee in addition to our big awning for it gets cold at dinnertime now. Between 3 a.m. and 9 a.m. it is pretty bitter; I wear a sweater and a pair of socks and a nightcap, in addition to pyjamas, now; two blankets on top and one underneath, and sometimes a greatcoat on for dinner!"

Both regiments then went their separate ways. Roger developed jaundice from lying out in the snow at Majuba Hill and was sent to hospital before he eventually rejoined his battalion, after missing the

Battle of Botha's Pass. At the end of 1900 the battalion's new quartermaster had not arrived, and "in addition to doing his work and my own I was given charge of a local supply depot" and had a small remount depot to take care of cattle and horses which had been driven in from Boer farms. But he "found time to organize the breaking-in of wild horses and to put up races for the troops" as well as playing polo. More unusually, Roger had the reputation of being a water diviner and he made use of his rod to find water when it was badly needed.

When applications were invited for the post of railway staff officer at Bloemfontein in December 1901, Roger put in for the job and got it – "a very good billet, I think". He wrote later that "I had always been interested in railways and thought this chance of getting experience would be useful. Bloemfontein was a big junction, but at that time there was only a single track through the Orange Free State, so train arrangements had to be worked out by means of a graph. Our work was always pretty hectic, especially at times when large troop movements were on." He commented in a letter written at the time that "the work is unlike any other job out here; it chiefly consists in being tactful, always polite, and never losing your temper!"

Geoffrey, meanwhile, had continued to be involved in actions against the Boers. In June 1900 they attempted to take a hill adjoining Botha's Pass with the Boers holding their fire until "we were within 300 yards of them, when they turned a *pom-pom* onto us, but our only casualties were one man killed and one wounded." He also spent a number of months garrisoning Vryheid where at times they faced plenty of Boer activity. In June, 400 Boers concentrated during the night within rifle range of the town and "there were constant rumours of impending attacks by the enemy. Louis Botha was said to be back at Watervaal, posts were reinforced and a church parade cancelled the following Sunday, but all remained quiet." Following these alarms much time was spent in sporadic destruction of Boer farms and in improving defences, using blockhouses and barbed wire. A detachment surrounded a farm some ten miles south of Vryheid, capturing five Boers, eight horses, ten trek oxen, ammunition and a great haul of chicken and geese. They also put in intense work strengthening defences around the town itself.

By then their brother Louis had also arrived in South Africa. He had studied at Keble College, Oxford for two years (1898-9) before joining the Queen's Regiment as a second lieutenant in June 1900 and then transferring to the Sherwood Foresters in May 1901. He served in South Africa from 1900 to 1902 and was involved in operations in Cape Colony, south of the Orange River and in the Transvaal.

Another side of this war is shown by Roger and Geoffrey's experiences with Boer leaders. On one occasion Roger had the Boer leader, De Wet, in his office for an hour between trains, to save him getting mobbed on the platform. Incidentally, some months earlier one of Roger's night patrols had killed one of De Wet's scouts carrying despatches and "when I went out at daybreak found he had two bullets in his forehead an inch apart – pretty good shooting! I then buried him and told a party to fill in the grave; whereupon a little cockney saluted and said 'Beg pardon, Sir, but e's got one of our greatcoats on; can I go in and get it out?'!"

Geoffrey also came across Boer leaders and their families. When the regiment first marched into Vryheid in January 1901 they found the people very friendly, including the Bothas. As he comments "it seems strange looking back how we received hospitality and played tennis with the nieces of the Boer commandant - Louis Botha – whilst the war was still in progress!" In April 1902 Louis Botha arrived at the station buildings and Geoffrey "sent him a box of chocolates for his young son". The following month, hearing that he was returning from a peace conference at Vereeniging, Geoffrey rode out to meet him and "saluting him I asked if I might take his photograph. He said "How long will it take?" and I replied "About 1800th of a second. He couldn't help smiling and gave his consent."

In March Geoffrey "had the honour and pleasure of looking after General Cheere-Emmett for 24 hours. It was indeed a pleasure, for though his captors told me that he had notified them of his determination to escape, I found him extremely interesting. To begin with, he was a great sportsman and had for some time been a collector of big game. He slept in a bed alongside mine, and we talked of our experiences – hunting and shooting in particular – until midnight. I had my revolver under my pillow and a lighted candle close at hand. Cheere begged me to put out the candle but I declined, considering it altogether too great a risk."

Geoffrey went down with dysentery again at the end of December 1901 and was sent to hospital. "The improvements since I was there two years ago (after Spion Kop) were tremendous! I had a room to myself, and, thanks to the new methods of dealing with dysentery, I was allowed to leave after six days."

Both brothers saw the effects of thunder and lightning. Roger had "quite an adventure when all the wagons of the column got bogged in a *vlei*.[32] Double-spanning hauled all mine out but one. I was determined to save it, and put all six spans – 96 oxen – on to the job. It did the trick, in spite of all the warnings of the conductors that it would mean pulling out the wheels and leaving the body of the wagon in the *vlei*." Geoffrey saw lightning set off all the mines by the south gun, split a big rock outside the mess HQ in two, seriously injure six men in the signallers' tent and kill two cats in the tent.

They also had time for more pleasurable pursuits. Roger took part in some amateur theatricals where he had some first-class coaching from a man who was running a touring company 'Hall's Australian Juveniles'. They were "a delightful lot of clever, unspoilt children" and he used to go to their performances and got to know the children. Geoffrey, being in a garrison town for the later part of the war, played cricket and tennis, won third prize in the 'animals race' in a gymkhana with a peacock, began collecting birds for his commanding officer's collection, rode his pony in steeplechases, and went fishing and shooting.

When the war came to an end, Roger put in for leave, but he was given a 'buff-slip' on which was written "Lieutenant Mott is permitted to proceed to England at his own expense, for three months!" As he commented "it seemed outrageous after so long a period of active service". He had to pay £60 for his passage.

Geoffrey did not reach Devon until the end of August. At the time of the cease fire he was the junior of the party of officers to take the surrender of the Boers and General Botha gave him his signature. He also got his highest score in a cricket match (62 not out), they had their first guest night since 1899, with the band playing, and he went on his final shoot. At sea on the way home they celebrated the coronation of Edward VII with champagne.

It was peacetime again and the brothers' lives were to follow different and yet similar paths. Roger did not fancy paying £60 for

---

[32] A vlei is a hollow in which rain collects, in this case due to a thunderstorm.

the return journey to South Africa. The result was that "I sent in my papers and stayed in England. It was probably a foolish decision, but I was young and foolish!"

CHAPTER EIGHT

RACING AND ARMY LIFE

Roger said that his decision to leave the army was probably foolish, but he was in a position to make it because of a fortunate series of inheritances, which brought him a number of properties, including those that remained from the estates built up by Charles' great-grandfather, William Mott, before his death in 1826.

In April 1887 Charles' father, William, in the final month of his life, wrote a letter to his eldest son Reverend William Kynaston Mott (Willie). "I wish to leave in writing, my expression of thanks to you for your great kindness shown to me during my hours of pain and sickness, and trouble. You have always been a good son to me. I could have wished to have left you married, and with a family, to carry on this place (Wall House, Lichfield) – but I do hope it may be arranged for the place not to be let, but carried on" with "your coming here at intervals and some of dear Charles' little boys" (Roger, Geoffrey and Louis).

Two years later, in September 1889, Willie, his eldest son and Charles' brother, dropped dead in the paddock at Derby racecourse, and, being still unmarried, his estates passed to his nephew Roger. This meant that, although so much of William Mott's original purchases before 1826 had by now been sold, Roger still inherited Wall House, Lichfield. He also inherited Spring Grove in Kent which had belonged to the Brett family. The last of the Bretts had married Anne Kynaston in 1798 and on her death it passed to her nephew, Roger Kynaston, Secretary to the MCC.[33] After his death he left it to his nephew, Willie, who passed it on to Roger.

In addition the manor and most of the village of Meysey Hampton in Gloucestershire, bought by William Mott, was left between Roger and his brothers, and their first cousins John and Elma, children of their aunt Henrietta Mott, and now living in Australia.[34] This included

---

[33] See Kynaston family tree p. 166
[34] See Mott family tree p. 162

an 800 acre farm let out to the Hobbs family, well-known breeders of Oxford Down sheep which produced a rent of £1,100 a year in the late 1870s. Roger bought the others out but, soon after returning from South Africa, realising that "the outgoings of the Kent and Gloucestershire properties were such that there was little income left, decided to sell both and only retain Wall. The tenants of Spring Grove farm and Meysey Hampton both bought their farms. For a time I kept on the house at Spring Grove, did it up and let it to my aunt 'Winkie', widow of Gerald Parlby, but in the end I sold it."[35]

On his return Geoffrey's immediate concerns were with a girl called Olive whom he had met at a 4 a.m. meet of the Dartmoor Otter Hounds, just before leaving for South Africa. When he fell into her arms on the platform at Ivybridge in August 1902, he had not seen her for three years. Olive's family, the Ellis' had a house adjoining the station and they "spent a very happy four hours before I tore myself away and dutifully made for the family at Oxford."

He found his stepmother Marian alone and took her up to London to join Roger and their sister, Alice. Two days later the brothers returned to Devon when they went to Manadon and looked up the Parlby family. They went hunting over the next few days and were joined by Olive and her two sisters and brother, Joe. But Geoffrey, when crossing the river Exe, met "the most sudden flood I have ever experienced. I was washed off my legs and had to swim for it. Not being a strong swimmer I had the greatest difficulty in reaching the bank and was only saved at the last minute by the gallant efforts of my future brother-in-law Joe Ellis."

In October he took Olive to Oxford to get to know the family during a week which included a Paderewski concert, listening to the Magdalen College Choir in the inner chapel, seeing a rugby match and going hunting. Shortly afterwards Geoffrey and Olive became formally engaged. In the spring of the following year he took her to Manadon to meet his Parlby relatives.

But before he could get married he had to work for the promotion exam which he had failed earlier. This time he was successful and this enabled him to go ahead and get married. At the end of the year he took Olive up to London for pre-wedding shopping and stayed first with Roger and then with his stepmother, Marian and sister

---

[35] For Meysey Hampton rents see Lichfield Record Office D546/19/4/1-4; for Aunt Winkie see Parlby family tree p. 164

Alice until Olive rejoined her own family for Christmas. In January 1905 Geoffrey entertained the whole Ellis family to lunch and then went to Manadon to prepare for the wedding. Roger, Alice and Marian dined with the Ellis family in Plymouth on the evening before the wedding and they were married in Plymouth before going to Exmoor for their honeymoon.

By then Roger had used the proceeds of his sales to move to Ampthill Grange in Bedfordshire where he became a JP in 1904. The reason for this purchase was that as he explains "I had always loved horses, and before the Boer war had begun to take an interest in the subject of breeding thoroughbreds. One of the few books I took out with me to South Africa dealt with the subject. I had bought a yearling called Royal Bess and it was in training at Newmarket. I had registered my racing colours – coffee, white collar and cuffs, green sleeves and cap. So I made up my mind to go in for breeding thoroughbreds."

Racing was very much in the family blood. John Mott, his great-grandfather, kept horses at his house in the Mansion House in the cathedral close at Lichfield, built by his father, William. When the house had to be sold on John's death, the bishop wittily remarked that he had "turned a stud into a study"! John also owned racehorses in the 1820s and 1830s. His grandson, Edward, says that he "kept a few brood mares on a farm close to Lichfield" and that he "used to have them trained at Hednesford on Cannock Chase" but described them as "unsuccessful brutes for the most part". Edward remembered best "an old chestnut, stone-blind, the dam of Goldfinder. This mare had been 'begged' from Lord Chesterfield, who would otherwise have had her shot. She bred one or two for my grandfather (John Mott), but nothing of any note. Goldfinder himself (who belonged to William Palmer) I saw win the Staffordshire Stakes on Whittington Heath, in my grandfather's nomination, in (I think) 1853. At any rate it was the very first race meeting I attended, as a very small boy, on a very rough pony."[36] Later he writes that "I escorted my grandfather (to the Grand National), who was 72, and a sad cripple from gout. I had a terrible job to get my old man back to Lichfield that evening."[37]

Edward's father, William, showed the same enthusiasm for racing. Edward writes that he "used to attend most of the principal

---

[36] A Mingled Yarn p. 264, 265. Three years later William Palmer, a surgeon, was hanged after being found guilty of poisoning by strychnine.
[37] A Mingled Yarn p. 274

William Mott – founder of the family fortunes

His son and Charles' grandfather, John Mott, in the uniform of the Staffordshire Yeomanry

John's wife Henrietta in an ermine cloak

John's son and Charles' father, William Mott, in the uniform of the Staffordshire Yeomanry

Charles' father, William Mott

Charles' mother, Louisa Mott

Charles' father William and his
second wife, Anna Maria Ward

Charles' eldest brother, Willie

Reverend John Hall Parlby –
the 'squarson' of Manadon

Gertrude Parlby –
Charles' first wife

(From left to right) Mildred (Millie) Parlby,
Winifred Parlby, Mrs
Parlby, Roger Mott on her knee and Willie
Mott. This picture was probably taken
when Roger was living with them while
Charles and Gertrude were in India

Charles' sister, Sissie who married
Arthur Coode

Charles' second wife, Marian Mott, with (from left to right) Louis, Alice, Geoffrey and Roger. The kilt that Louis is wearing and Alice's doll are referred to on Page 52

Charles Mott in uniform

Charles' first wife, Gertrude Mott

Charles' brother Edward 'the bad boy of the family'

Roger Mott as a child

Geoffrey Mott as a young child

Roger Mott

Geoffrey Mott in uniform at the
time of the Boer War

Louis Mott prior to his departure
for Canada in 1904

Their sister Alice Mott

Roger's wife Helen at Wall House, Lichfield with Sylvia and Charles

Roger Mott in uniform with (from left to right) Sylvia, Antony and Charles at Bath 1914-15

(From left to right) Geoffrey and Roger Mott at the meet of the Culmstock Otter Hounds at the Cross Keys Inn, near Taunton, 1919

Roger Mott, Master of the Culmstock Otter Hounds, 1949

Geoffrey Mott in military
uniform with medals

Geoffrey's wife, Olive

Geoffrey Mott in the uniform of the
Dartmoor Otter Hounds, blowing his
Gallipoli horn

(From left to right) Roger,
Geoffrey and Louis Mott

meetings, in company with a party of friends – the Doncaster party held together for a great many years – but he never owned a race-horse."[38] On one occasion when Edward was due to return to Sandhurst he "came to my bedside very early and confided to me that, so far, he had had 'a very bad Goodwood'. 'In fact' he added 'if The Wizard doesn't win today, I shall be hard hit'."[39] Roger commented that "I fancy he was rather too fond of racing and died poor."

Edward was taken by William, his father, to Goodwood for the first time in July 1861 when "through the hospitality of an over-indulgent parent, I made one of a jovial party at the Bedford Hotel, Brighton, who journeyed to the ducal park and back again daily. To a boy of 17, a regime of turtle and other savoury meats, washed down with sparkling wines, was no common or unwelcome experience."[40] After his return from India, Edward soon drifted into what he described as a "habitual follower of the sport of kings" and became a confirmed gambler.[41]

But Roger was to be more successful, both in racing terms and financially, than his ancestors. He looked out for a farm with suitable soil and bought Ampthill Grange, where his stepmother, Marian, and his sister Alice came "to keep house for me" and where they were visited by Marian's sisters Alice and Louise and her brother Richard and his wife. Roger kept on buying until he had a dozen mares and his yearlings were then put up for sale each year at Newmarket. "In 1904 Millbrook failed to make her reserve so I sent her to Sadler (at Newmarket) to be trained. Next year she won a two-year-old race at Alexandra Park. Unfortunately, a big betting-man got wind of the fact that she had been well-tried and backed her down to 5-2 before the stable could get its money on."

At the sales in 1905 he was left with two yearlings which he sent to Sadler again. Ampthill won a nice race at Lingfield, and (his most successful horse) Offer one at Leicester and one at Newmarket. "This was the Plantation Stakes, a good-class race. The mare won cleverly and her price was 20-1. I had a good win and that paid all my racing expenses for the year."

The following year, Roger decided to train his own horses and

---

[38] A Mingled Yarn p. 264
[39] A Mingled Yarn p. 64
[40] A Mingled Yarn p. 63
[41] A Mingled Yarn p. 276

got hold of a training establishment at Royston. "I used to spend the week at Royston and the weekends at Ampthill, driving backwards and forwards with my trainer's hack in a light cart. What fun it all was!" Offer ran at Epsom in June 1907 in the Stewards' Handicap, which was worth £1,000. "This was the race after the Derby, and over the same course as that race and the Oaks. She won very easily; so I had the thrill of leading her in, amid congratulations from various friends. She won at 100 to 12. A neighbour from Royston – quite a poor man – had the temerity to put £100 on! He insisted on standing me a good dinner that night, and I told him he should never bet again." Geoffrey wrote in his diary "Offer won Stewards' Handicap at Epsom *(£1,000)*!!!"

The following year Roger moved his string of horses to Ilsley and bought an old steeplechaser Marron Glacé at Tattersalls for £60 to lead the work. "We soon started winning, Ampthill at Newbury and Best China at Warwick. Offer was disappointing but that was probably because I was too ambitious and entered her for the Hunt Cup at Ascot instead of in the City and Suburban at Epsom. She had shown a liking for that course, and was wonderful downhill, in fact I believe she would have won the 1907 Oaks." She was entered for the race but "as she came down in the road and cut her knees badly, a week before the forfeit was to be declared, I took her out of the race."

Offer's best performance in 1908 was at Newmarket where she was only beaten by the best horse of his year, Radium, by a head. Radium belonged to Leonard Rothschild and the jockey, Lynham, who Roger engaged each time to ride Offer, asked if he could ride for Rothschild instead. Roger agreed if he got a first-class substitute, which he did. Roger says that "it was a thrilling race, and in the trainers' stand everyone thought Offer had won. After the race Halsey told me he would have won, had he known how good the mare was downhill; and Lynham said he could have won on her!"

By now Roger "had begun sending mares to some of the best stallions at 300 guinea fees. I used to take the mares away myself, and so saw some famous studs – Sandringham, Welbeck. During a visit to Dick Marsh (the King's trainer) at Heath House, Newmarket, I saw an old mare called Granny with a lovely foal. The owner was broke, and could not pay his bill, and Marsh offered me the mare and foal for £200. I accepted and sold the foal next year for £500."

"Things were going well with me until a mare came back from Newmarket and developed pleuropneumonia, which spread to all the young stock; half of them died and the rest were permanently affected, so I decided to clear out and sold everything."

"Actually I did not do too badly with the horses - 24 mares cost £2,954 and were sold for £7,020. Stud fees cost £3,427; yearlings were sold for £1,463, and the unsold ones won £2,336, a total of £3,799. And what a lot of fun I had!"

Geoffrey, in contrast, after five months of leave following his return from South Africa in 1902, "the most enjoyable I ever experienced", and after attending medical boards, received orders to join his regiment. He now had 12 years peace-time soldiering "most of it was exceedingly dull and tedious, and indeed only tolerable for the numerous spells of leave sandwiched into it. I never hesitated to put in for leave as frequently as I dared."

At first he was posted to Dover, where he took the opportunity "of making for Wye for a day or two to look around the property, owned by my brother, called Spring Grove." He also went to see his brother's brood mares when he first began breeding thoroughbreds and went with him to Epsom. When he was on his first course of musketry at Hythe, Colonel Munro, who was inspecting the squads, "came round to mine, and was handed a list he said 'which of you is Mott?' When I saluted he asked 'which are you Roger, Geoffrey or Louis?' and when I replied 'Geoffrey' he said 'many a time I have had you over my knees and spanked you!' He sent for me after the parade and told me that he had been my father's subaltern in the Queen's Regiment and was often in our house when we were small." He also gave Geoffrey great encouragement and he enjoyed every minute of the musketry course.

When Geoffrey first did a tour of duty at the depot in Warrington, Olive was able to spend some time there, as she had friends nearby, but, after their honeymoon, they found rooms near the depot. They both attended the Aintree Grand National and "enjoyed it in great comfort, the depot having a room in the grandstand".

When they moved to Aldershot, the officers had so much time on their hands, that Geoffrey was in charge of the cricket and "when asked to enter for the Aldershot Tournament, I readily agreed. I had not considered consulting my brother officers and to my astonishment they criticized my action quite harshly, reasoning that it was hopeless our competing in view of our having no wicket to practice on!" When the critical day arrived "great was the grumbling as we made for the club, but fortunately everyone asked to play turned up in the end. We had drawn the cup holders who had two first-class county players." Winning the toss, "I put them in and we dismissed them for the low total of 118. We replied with 120 for 6. I went in first and luckily knocked up 55. Alas I had made one blunder, or rather omission." Geoffrey had played a useful bowler who had just been seconded to the Army Ordnance Corps, and so was ineligible, even though he had not yet left the regiment. The opposition sportingly suggested a replay when "to our amazement we beat them again, though by only five runs". Unfortunately in the next round they lost by a similarly narrow margin.

In September, the divisional manoeuvres took place near Lavington Park. As mess president, Geoffrey, together with Captain Dawson, called on their host Mr Buchanan, the chairman of the company that produced White Horse whisky. He gave them a great welcome and showed them his racing stud. The result was that, although the six days of manoeuvres were "fairly strenuous", for Geoffrey and Captain Dawson, "Mr Buchanan hit us off every day at the luncheon interval and fed us right royally on shrimps in aspic and similar delicacies washed down with vintage wines, and we ended the manoeuvres with champagne and sandwiches on the grandstand at Goodwood." Not only that, but on the final day Mr Buchanan said to them "You are dining with me tonight". And when we explained that only the general and battle commanders had been invited, he replied that he could ask who he liked!

In March 1907 Geoffrey crossed swords with his commanding officer. "A corporal came up before him for drunkenness, and, wishing him to receive a more severe punishment than he was authorized to impose, he had him tried by regimental court martial, of which I was appointed president. I found the evidence insufficient to convict, so I acquitted him. The colonel was furious, but instead of talking the case over with me personally, he directed the adjutant to send me an official letter, demanding an explanation of my action. Being determined to clear myself of blame, I despatched a full account of the case by express train to Plymouth, to my father-in-law (who was Town Clerk of Plymouth), and he, consulting with a military lawyer there, sent a reply to me by train the same day. I accordingly lost no time in sending my official reply to my commanding officer. This correspondence lasted for three days ending in a complete triumph for me, although no apology was forthcoming! He told the adjutant that 'he would let the matter drop'! I was disgusted."

In June he went on a mounted infantry course and he and Olive found excellent rooms. Most of the officers played polo but Geoffrey decided to play cricket instead which he thoroughly enjoyed. Mounted manoeuvres took place in September in which they covered over 200 miles in nine days starting at Wargrave and Henley. When he tried to gallop round the enemy's left flank and engage them, he was charged by the cavalry, but it was ruled that they were both 'out of bounds'! While on manoeuvres "I used to control my company with the hunting horn. If I gave a long blast the sections had to come up at a trot for orders. If I doubled my horn the section officers had to gallop to receive an urgent order." When Geoffrey was asked what on earth was going on, he said that "in my brigade the brigadier always used to summon his battalion commanders with the hunting horn and I thought it would be an excellent idea to try it on my command." The colonel said that it was a 'capital idea'.

Geoffrey took over as adjutant of the South Lancashire Regiment at Warrington at the end of the year and, with Olive, he settled into a house on the Cheshire side of the Manchester ship canal. One day he flushed a woodcock in the small garden lying in a border of climbing nasturtiums! His first engagements included an official dinner given for Haldane, the Secretary of State for War and a dinner at the club for 20 guests, followed by the annual prize giving for the fourth battalion. "I had to announce the prize winners on the stage, which was immediately afterwards occupied by the famous comedian George Robey, who was particularly amusing as the Mayor" – he was attending as a guest!

At the end of the year Geoffrey acted in an invasion play called *A Stitch in Time*. This was taken all over Lancashire, including Liverpool and Manchester. He comments that "it went down especially well in Preston: the only place where it was received without applause, or even a hiss, was Rochdale!"

Roger was also involved in theatricals and Alice's "great friend Nell Cumberlege, came to act in them". The two of them were at school together and Helen (Nell) had stayed at Ampthill Grange on two occasions in October 1906 and then again at the beginning of 1907. But it was when she was staying at the beginning of 1908 that "I proposed to her after the last performance on 21 January and was accepted".

Roger and Helen were married at Lindfield in Sussex on 30 April 1908. She was the eldest daughter of Henry Mordaunt Cumberlege and his wife Blanche *née* Fenwick of Walstead Place. It was reported that "the villagers of Walstead and Walstead Place had been busy for some time in preparing for the happy ceremony, and the result was a perfect display of flags, bunting and other decorations." After a fortnight's honeymoon in Venice, they settled at Ilsley, going riding and racing together until he had to give up racing. They then moved to Ampthill for a short time before going to live in the family house that Roger had inherited at Wall, near Lichfield. His stepmother, Marian, and his sister Alice moved to The Old Vicarage at Cuddesdon, near Oxford, where Marian lived swathed in black and surrounded by her parrot and her dogs.

CHAPTER NINE

WALL HOUSE, SERVICE IN IRELAND AND THE NATIONAL
SERVICE LEAGUE

Wall House had been let, with all its contents, since Roger's grandfather, William, married for the second time and went to live in St Leonards, and its condition had suffered as a result. In 1897 a list was drawn up of contents that had gone missing and of rooms requiring whitening and colouring, many of which also had broken panes, as well as repairs needed to outbuildings and the gardens. Roger says that there was still "a good deal to be done to the house" and that repairs were "not quite finished when we left Ampthill; so we moved into Pool House, Lichfield for a few days. The house was empty so we put in a minimum of furniture and suffered from the cold! It was formerly the house of my two old great-aunts, Emily and Georgie Mott."

Roger and Helen finally moved into Wall in January 1909 and were very happy there "and quite expected to be there for the rest of our days". Roger bought Wall Hall, "another nice house close to ours" and let it out. They also had "a brougham and a ralli cart to go about in, until I bought our first motor car a Humber 12 in 1910. I knew nothing about cars, but drove it back alone from the works at Coventry, and then engaged a chauffeur to look after it."

Wall is on the site of a small Romano-British settlement *Leocetum*, at the junction of the old Watling Street and the Fosseway. Roger came to an agreement with the North Staffordshire Field Club to excavate the site and their reports show that he was "quite indefatigable in his devotion to it, digging with his own hands where difficulties arose, and watching minutely the results of his workmen's picks and spades." They uncovered the foundations of the bath house, whose remains were more complete than any others of a similar nature in Britain, as well as a second building which proved to be an ancient Roman villa. "Everything that turned up was watched and recorded" and the "finds" were exhibited at Wall. Roger invited "distinguished experts" on the subject to give further advice and the work proceeded under his "constant attendance and supervision" until he became involved in the work of the National Service League.

There were changes in both families in these years. Roger and Helen's eldest child, Charles, was born at Wall in March 1909 and Roger's stepmother, Marian, and her sister Alice came to Wall to see the baby in May, the same month that Geoffrey and Olive's first child, John, was born.

There had also been big changes in the life of their younger brother, Louis. After serving in South Africa and China, he left the army and Geoffrey saw him off from Liverpool as he sailed to Canada in June 1904. He took with him a number of travelling dog kennels, mainly containing spaniels, and settled in Alix, Alberta, where his uncle, Edward Parlby, lived. Here he became a rancher in Lamerton, until he took the decision to enter the church and became a deacon in 1907, serving as curate in the parish of St Monica, Lamerton with St Pancras, Alix. He did not return to England until 1909, when he enrolled at the Bishops' Theological College in Cheshunt.

In September of that year Geoffrey and Olive went to Cuddesdon to stay with his stepmother, Marian, and sister Alice. But while they were out hunting with the South Oxfordshire "Alice, who was driving Olive, was taken ill and the following day was removed to the Acland Nursing Home in Oxford and operated on for appendicitis". A week later the surgeon assured Geoffrey that she was out of danger and he and Olive returned to Warrington. But two days later he got a telegram saying "Alice's condition critical - come at once". He reached the nursing home by 7.30 a.m. the following morning. "The darling sister knew me at once and sent her love to 'Olive and baby John'." Roger arrived in time to see her at 11.15 a.m. but, by the time Louis arrived at 12.20 p.m., he was "just too late" to see her conscious. "At 12.37 p.m. after a great and noble fight for life she passed away" aged 28. The three brothers made arrangements for the funeral and Geoffrey took Olive to see his stepmother. The body was escorted to Cuddesdon "where we placed her in the dining room" before her funeral.

Roger and Helen had two more children before the outbreak of war in 1914 – Sylvia who was born in April 1911 and Antony in March 1913, while Geoffrey and Olive's second son Raymond was born a day after the declaration of war on 5 August 1914. Louis, meanwhile, was ordained as a priest in 1910, and became a curate at St Faith's, Brentford before moving to South Molton in Devon in 1912.

Geoffrey handed over his adjutancy at Warrington after three years, at the end of October 1910, and rejoined his regiment in Ireland, where he served for the next three years. Finding suitable places for the family to live and suitable servants was always a problem. At the beginning of 1911 he and Olive took Castle View, Butterant "of a truth a chilly house!!" for six weeks. But within ten days they were looking for something more permanent. In doing so they were helped by being able to get around on the motor bike – a Premier - that he had bought in England and had shipped over with a sidecar. They looked over a house with "very dingy bedrooms" and with the "sanitary arrangements highly doubtful!" But a week later they were shown a cottage by Mr Harold Barry, known as Kilcolman House, at Ballyronare and came to an agreement with him over "all details for repair and alteration". Having visited Cork with Barry to choose a kitchen range and drawing room grate and having had a further discussion with him about alterations to the house, they found it "alive with workmen" and made frequent visits to inspect progress. By the beginning of March they moved their furniture in, filled the lamps, scrubbed the tables and cleaned the house while more shelves were put in. They arranged for a cleaner to come in and set aside a room for a cook. But, despite all the workmen, the end product was "*very* roughly finished" and had "*no* convenience of *any* sort!!!" Nevertheless they signed an agreement with Barry to the effect that they would take the house from March to October for £1 a month.

The new cook, Mary Ryan, arrived two days after they moved in, by which time they were busy making it homely by hanging pictures and putting down carpets. Workmen were still carrying out repairs at the end of the month when they were fixing the gate and painting the exterior of the windows. Olive gave Mary Ryan a month's notice at the beginning of May and by the middle of June they were looking for a replacement. They heard of four possible cooks, and took on Christina McLoughlin.

However, by the end of September they were packing up again, as the regiment had to move to the Curragh, and they handed over the keys to Mr Barry early in October. They now had to look for a new house and found some "at *fabulous* rents", but settled on taking Thornton House from Captain Morley. They planned to move in at the beginning of the following year, after their leave in England, but found it "damp and *not nearly* ready". A few days later the papering of the bathroom was just being completed and a servant's room was ready. Geoffrey then spent several days with some of his soldiers, getting the dining and drawing rooms scrubbed out and the kitchen and scullery working and generally making sure that everything was ready, before Olive came over from England at the end of January. He had planned for Marion Murphy to be engaged as a cook, but she let them down at the last minute, and Lizzie Ward was taken on. The following year saw a spate of cooks – Kate McGrath arrived but was given her notice two weeks later "too much 'the old soldier' and impertinent". A few days later she scalded her foot and had to see Dr Thunder who sent her to Drogheda Hospital! Winnie McDonald then arrived as a replacement but was given her notice a few days later, to be replaced by Nellie Corcoran. The dampness in the house also continued to be a problem and when they returned after leave in England they found it "*black* with mildew!!"

Another necessity in Ireland was to have a means of transport. At first this was provided by the motor bike and sidecar. Journeys were always hazardous and repairs were frequently needed. In one month, the right hand fork split clean through and was hanging on a thread and new forks had to be sent from Coventry. It misfired which meant taking the carburettor to pieces, the cause being a short circuit of the sparking plug. And the clutch had to be dismantled and sent to England, along with the rear wheel, to Bowden's of Ivybridge, which took two weeks to return. By July he had driven 2,675 miles on the bike, but in October he decided to sell it and buy a car.

When he was over in England on leave, staying with Roger at Wall, he heard of a four seater eight horse power Rover, belonging to a doctor in Uttoxeter, who had just died, which he bought for £90. This was thought to be a 'great bargain' as it was a March 1919 model. But, when the new car arrived at Ivybridge, it did so "ignominiously drawn by a Lyons' Tea motor van, having broken down on Haldon Hill in the dark in a terrific storm!", so it was sent to Bowden's for repair. As soon as it was returned, Geoffrey, Olive and Willie Bowden went out for a lesson, but "just as I was getting on quite admirably, there was a terrific clank and then we found the connecting rod and later a cylinder rod broken." A week later the car was repaired again but, when trying the Bickleigh Bridge hill with three up, it proved too steep and "I had to get out at one point and walk".

Nevertheless, having overcome these initial difficulties, the car was shipped over to Ireland and a motor shed of galvanized iron was constructed at their house, although it took over two weeks to erect! In June he gave Olive her first lesson in driving the car, but the following month, on their way to Dublin, Geoffrey had a "most unfortunate accident in Naas when my car went over an old man Matt Carr. I was climbing a slight hill in low gear after stopping at a shop" when Carr "suddenly stepped off the pavement only a few yards in front of me. I swerved to the right to avoid him, but he suddenly ran across, and though I braked at once he backed into my radiator and fell down. He was carried into the nearest house and I followed, much disturbed, but an Irish doctor eased my mind by telling me 'He'll be alright, he is always on the drink but he never eats meat. He is a bog worker – don't worry'!" He visited him in hospital several times where they found his jawbone was broken, and he proved to be a "decent old chap, and declined any idea of compensation, though I believe a grasping cousin got something out of my insurance company!"

Another feature of life in Ireland was the large number of cricket matches played by the regiment each summer in June, July and August. In 1911 he played 20 matches, with their team's biggest score being 368 against Tipperary County and Geoffrey's highest score being 64 against the East Surrey Regiment. In 1912 they went on tour to Cork for the cricket week, but rain meant no cricket was possible for the first two days. When playing against the Curragh, his new ten horse power four cylinder Darracq was delivered just before the end of the match, and he drove Olive home in it; he found it very comfortable.

So much bowling in cricket helped to bring on sciatica in his shoulder, which gave him a lot of trouble. In May 1912 he stayed in the Queen Alexandra Military Hospital in London for two weeks, which involved radiant heat baths at 110 degrees, 'high frequency' treatment, which consisted of a thick glass needle charged with electricity run over the nerve, an electric vibrator and massages. All this treatment did not affect his shooting ability as shortly afterwards he won the Officer's Cup and his company the best shooting company.

An event which took the regiment to Belfast, was the need to keep order during the visit of Winston Churchill in February 1912. Geoffrey went to the Grand Central Hotel where he met Ashmead Bartlett, a correspondent of the Daily Telegraph who dined them well. On the day of the visit itself they marched to the Royal Victoria

Hospital, where they stayed until 4 p.m. All "went off peacefully enough, though it was reported that his (Churchill's) car was turned over on its side whilst he was in the hall." The regiment then moved to the Brookfield weaving factory where the girl workers had to come down a staircase and pass through them at the end of their day's work. "Major Carlyon was standing Napoleon-like with arms folded, with his usual rather fierce expression" when "a hefty girl caught him by the waist, lifted him up and kissed him on both cheeks! I must have looked rather startled (though about to burst out laughing) because when she turned to me she said 'You're too fiercesome looking'!"

Two other incidents involving local Irishmen deserve mention. One morning, when fetching his dog back from a farm, Geoffrey learnt that the farmer, Mr Burke's father, had just died which led to a request to view the corpse as well as to join them in drinking whisky. The following day there were a countless number of ass-carts at the well-attended funeral. The other was when he had to appear in court at Naas to give a character reference for a soldier who had broken a plate glass window. When Judge Gibson, who was presiding at the Assizes, heard Geoffrey's name "he asked me whether I was any relation of a Mott he had met in Galway in the 1870s. 'Son, your honour' said I, on which he stood up and shook hands saying 'Delighted to meet you Sir'."

In his last few months in Ireland Geoffrey was able to go fishing on a number of occasions and Dr Blown "put me up to the good places and methods on the Liffey". When he asked Lord Fitzgerald for a day's fishing he got permission to fish the Greese for the season and Percy La Touche let him fish his two-mile stretch of the Liffey. Geoffrey also attended both days of the Punchestown Races.

But it was now time to leave Ireland. Geoffrey sold the car for £170, after giving the prospective purchaser three lessons in driving it, and spent three days packing up and seeing the family off in August 1913. He left a month later.

While living at Wall, Roger had been appointed secretary for the Staffordshire branch of the National Service League. "This meant visiting every town and village in the county preaching the doctrine that every young man should undergo a short period of military training to fit himself to defend his country, if the need should arise." He also had to organize dinner-hour meetings at the various works, the largest being held in the Victoria Hall, Hanley in the Potteries, attended by about 2,000 people. Unfortunately the principal speaker, Lord Curzon, "dropped a bad brick" when he said "now in your trade here ..." and was seen to whisper to the Mayor 'what is it?'"

However, the league propaganda did not seem to be making enough headway, so the president, Lord Roberts, started a 'campaign committee', headed by Fred Browning, a man "with a great amount of drive" who had been educated at Roger's old school, Wellington College. "He arranged for 'Bobs' (Lord Roberts) to address really big meetings in the largest towns, one of which was Wolverhampton in March 1913. Browning sent a man named Percy Creed to help me to prepare for this meeting which gave me no end of work." But Roger's organizational skills were again shown to good effect. "We took the drill hall and filled it with 4,000 men – the names and addresses of all being recorded, for follow-up purposes." At the same time "there was an overflow meeting of 3,000 men, and Bobs' speech was relayed on a screen in an open square. Bobs was wonderful; he learned his speech by heart and never made a mistake!" "Next day I arranged for a meet of the Albrighton Hounds at Colonel Tom Hickman's house, Wergs Hall, where Bobs was staying and about 5,000 people turned out to see him. Then we had a lunch, to which about a dozen of the richest people in the district were invited – after which we did our best to 'put our hands into their pockets'!" Roger's second son, Antony, had been born the night of the meeting and, after telling Bobs, "the kind man handed me a cheque for £100 for the boy."

However, within the organization itself there was a lot of friction between the 'special committee' and the old league officials, and "as I had begun to feel that the methods of the latter were much too slow and amateurish, I resigned from the secretaryship." Roger left Wall in May 1913 and moved to Northumberland as he had become Master of the Northern Counties Otter Hounds and he spent the summer of 1913 based at Alnmouth. While there he was asked by the 'special committee' to organize five large meetings for the league. "Lord Percy – later the Duke of Northumberland – addressed the Hull meeting."

Fred Browning then "wrote to me, saying that Bobs felt the league organization wanted overhauling and would I think it over and report. This I did, suggesting an organization by large areas, with picked well-paid men as area-organisers. It appeared that the same question had been put to the chief organiser of the Liberal Party, who came to the same conclusions as mine: so Browning telegraphed for me to come to London, as a result of which I was asked to take over the secretaryship of the league."

This meant that Roger had to resign his mastership of the Northern Counties Otter Hounds, and move to Holly Bank, Lindfield and then to a house called 'Limehurst' at Hayward's Heath in Sussex in May 1914, so that he could travel each day to the London office of the National Service League at 72 Victoria Street.

While Roger was concentrating on the National Service League, Helen was bringing up the children. She contributed to a book of recipes and household hints, edited by her mother Blanche Cumberlege from their house, Walstead Place, and she came up with the title for the book *Lindfield Fare*, which is a *jeu de mots* on the ancient 'fair' well-known to all Sussex folk, held at Lindfield each August. This book went into two editions, 1912 and 1914, and raised money to pay off the debt on the village hall. In the book there are contributions from Helen's parents, brothers and sisters, from Roger, from his stepmother, Marian, at Cuddesdon, from his aunt Sissie Coode, from Mrs Parlby and from the cook at 'Wall'.

While Roger was working in London, his chairman was Lord Newton. "He once said to me: 'A good chairman leaves all he can to his secretary, who will not bother him unless a matter is really urgent; if it is, the chairman will see him, even if he is in his bath!' (I once hauled Lord Newton out of the House of Lords, to discuss an urgent matter)."

"We had a most distinguished lot of men on our committee, the best of whom was Lord Milner. I remember an occasion when there was a most stormy general meeting of the league, when Milner calmed it down with a masterly, tactful speech. We got some big businessmen onto the committee, but the politicians of the day were very difficult, though I believe Lloyd-George was in favour of National Service. We had a clever man to collect big money; he got Walter Morrison, a northern millionaire, to give £4,000 after a big meeting. Next day Morrison added another £6,000 – and exactly a year afterwards, our man had the cheek to write and say 'Your subscription for the coming year is now due' and the old sportsman coughed up another £10,000!"

In the process of being national secretary "I got to know Bobs well – 'The Little Man', we called him." Roger writes that it was a great privilege having so much to do with him. "I must mention two of his characteristics. One was his curious antipathy to cats; he always knew if one was in the room, even if he could not see it, and it upset him in some way. We always had to search a hall most carefully if he was going to speak. The other was his ability to fall asleep instantly and awake after a fixed period. I travelled with him once from St Pancras to Bedford, in a special coach – a journey of just an hour. Soon after we started he said 'I think I'll have a nap' and asked what time we were due at Bedford. I said 'One o'clock and I'll wake you five minutes beforehand.' 'You need not do that' he replied 'I shall wake myself.' He lay down and fell asleep in a moment. As we were running down the incline between Ampthill and Bedford at 80 miles an hour, I watched him – sleeping like a child, and exactly at 12.55 he woke!"

"I spent a delightful weekend with him once at 'Englemere', Ascot. He used to be up at six, and go through all his letters, sorting them out into the various organizations with which he was concerned. At nine, he read family prayers in his tiny chapel in the house, and after breakfast I went to his library, to go through the National Service League business."

Roger concluded that "the reorganization of the league came too late. It used to be said that it took 20 years to drive a new idea into an Englishman's head – and we had not the time. I shall always believe that, had we got National Service going, Germany would not have gone to war."

When war did break out "I remember Bobs coming into the office and saying 'well Mott this is the end of the NSL' and that he had offered the services of our office to the War Office. He also asked me to attend to all his correspondence. Each morning he arrived at the office, punctually at ten, and his men brought in a suitcase containing the letters. These I sorted myself, and answered any that I could; at six in the evening 'The Little Man' came in and took away any that I thought he must attend to himself."

The first job that they had at the War Office was to sift all their letters. "A lorry would come round three or four times a day filled with sacks of letters, which we sorted and sent back. We got a lot of men in to help, and organized them into squads of about a dozen, in various rooms, some of them outside the office itself. The War Office was a swarming hive of people, each department overflowing into the corridors. Another job they sent us was to sort out the hundreds of applications for jobs as interpreters. We made a lovely card-index of these, and sent it back only to be told that it was not understood – for apparently the War Office did not then use any card-indexing system!"

"One day I was asked if we could help by finding old non-commissioned officers; so I asked for a letter, signed by Lord Kitchener, and got it reproduced and sent all over the country through our area-organizers."

"Bobs issued appeals for saddles, and for field glasses, which produced floods of those things, and more work for us all. I had a stamp specially cut for Bobs' signature; it was so good that many of the recipients believed it to be his own writing, and framed the latter containing it!"

But "by the end of September 1914 our work for the War Office came to an end, and I was free to join the army again. The league was very good to me, and paid half my salary 'for the duration'; and "'The Little Man' presented me with a lovely, engraved cigarette case, which he had got in Paris." Soon afterwards he died from pneumonia, which he contracted at the Front, when visiting the Indian troops. Roger "attended the funeral service at St Paul's, and sat next to the Garter King at Arms and opposite, and quite close to, the King and Queen."

At the end of 1913 Geoffrey planned to leave the army and returned from leave to Collingbourne Ducis and 'The Chestnuts' "for the closing days of my soldiering career". By the beginning of March 1914 he put in for two months' leave, pending his retirement from 1 June, but the interview did not go well and his commanding officer persuaded the brigadier "to refuse my leave!!!" He thus had to carry out company training and a musketry course until the middle of May when they held a farewell dinner for him. Two days later he went to the "barracks for the last time!!"

In March he and Olive had taken a house at Ashburton called Greenaway Lodge which they had first seen at the end of December and considered "right in the town and not enough garden". But they arranged for repairs to be carried out and by the middle of May it looked "*very* much improved with new paint and wallpapers". They moved their furniture in and spent the next few weeks getting things as they wanted them. Geoffrey also started work on the garden "syringing my roses which are eaten up by greenfly with 'Cirenpol' and soft soap and putting soot on my sweet peas", as well as weeding beds and putting in bedding plants.

There were visits from Roger and Helen in May and from their stepmother in June, both staying at 'The Golden Lion'. Louis joined Marian, Geoffrey and Olive for two days before Marian left for Cuddesdon and Louis for South Molton. At the beginning of August the nurse arrived and four days later their second son Raymond was born. But by then the normality of life had been shattered by the news that war had been declared and Geoffrey wrote in his diary "I suppose I shall be ordered to Warrington soon".

CHAPTER TEN

THE FIRST WORLD WAR – 1914-1915

Quite soon after the war began Roger was offered a job by Ivo Vesey, who had joined the Queen's Regiment on the same day and was now working at the War Office. Roger had to refuse, as he was already so busy with the War Office work being carried out by the National Service League staff, which Vesey did not know about. He later discovered that the job he had been offered was a lieutenant colonel's appointment in counter-espionage, which as he says "would have been most interesting".

Unfortunately, by the time that he was free to join the army and was able to contact Vesey again, this post was no longer available and so he offered Roger a position as brigade major in the New Army, giving him a choice of several brigades. "None of them contained a 'Queen's' battalion, so I selected one which had a Devon battalion – the Devon's and the Queen's always having been such good friends, before and after the Boer War."

Roger comments that "conditions when I joined were chaotic", but his organizational and logistical experience, which he now put to good use as a staff officer, rapidly had an effect. He got hold of a first-class ex-army clerk, "wired to the National Service League office for a typewriter and quantities of stationery and went to Salisbury and bought all manner of things for the troops. They had not even got spades with which to dig latrines!" He had joined the 79th Infantry Brigade at Sherrington, near Codford in Wiltshire, which consisted of the 10th Devons, well-run by Colonel Ellicombe, whom he knew; the Duchy of Cornwall Light Infantry under "a gallant old man" Colonel Verschoyle; the 7th Wilts under Colonel Rocke "a rum fellow – a stern disciplinarian, but most obstinate"; and the 12th Hants not well-run by Colonel Walker. Overall in charge was General Fisher, "an elderly Ghurka, quite past his work. He smoked endless cigarettes and was terribly nervous of a horse!"

"Each battalion was allocated an area, but Rocke would not keep to his, and wandered with his battalion into that of the 78th Brigade, to the annoyance of their brigadier. So I sent Rocke a memorandum 'Thou shalt not covet thy neighbour's area, nor that of his Worcester's nor his Gloucester's, nor his Ox and Berks, nor anything that is his'! (Those were battalions of the 78th Brigade). Copies were sent to that brigade, and to divisional headquarters – to their great delight; and the matter was closed satisfactorily."

Roger had his own car and drove the general everywhere. He arranged a room in a farmhouse as an office for himself and his clerk and they were billeted at Fisherton Delamare House where they were "entertained wonderfully" by Mrs Newall. But by November 1914, with a lot of heavy rain, the conditions for the brigades became very flooded and the men, who were in bell-tents, "suffered severely". As brigade major, Roger had to visit towns and make arrangements for the troops to be billeted there. He put the Wilts into Marlborough, the Hampshire's into Basingstoke and the Devon's and Cornwall's into Bath.

When Roger went to Bath he "noticed no end of empty houses in Pulteney Street, so he went to an estate agent and arranged to take the lot at £1 a house a week. I got some builders to refit the basements for lavatory and washing purposes, and each house accommodated a platoon. This came out much cheaper than if the troops had been billeted. I took a large house for brigade headquarters, and brought the family to live there in November 1914. The general lived in the Pulteney Hotel."

The country around Bath proved very suitable for training. The man who was sent to carry out instruction in musketry brought his own car, which he preferred to be driven by someone else, so Roger "had a lot of fun with it". When the brigade was mounted Roger was sent "a topping dun cob, which I called Nunky; I think the remount officer confused me with Tom Mott, a famous polo-player"! Roger picked out a very quiet horse for the general "but he never rode it if it could be helped". When the time came for medicals before the brigade was to be sent to France, the general was 'retired' as he "was quite unfit for active service – indeed I had run the brigade up to then." He was replaced by Brigadier-General Poole who was a "first-class fighting man".

At the end of August 1914 Geoffrey received his orders to go to the depot at Warrington where he found "swarms of plain clothes recruits scattered all over the square drilling". The following day he took 136 men, a "noisy and dirty gang", to join Kitchener's Army at Tidworth – the 6th Battalion South Lancashire Regiment. He took over D company and received 100 more men "unclothed and *filthy*" from the depot. Everyone was enlisted into Kitchener's Army, including Bayley who had been kicked out of the Lancashire Regiment a year or two before. Described by Geoffrey as "that vulgar lump of humanity" he turned up at the barracks "looking coarser than ever" with his hair shaved off. But he was able to join the Hampshire's and was made a sergeant. Geoffrey's comment was 'Ugh!!' But the men of his company were knocked into shape by hours of training each day from 6 a.m. until 4.30 p.m. and aunt Sissie sent a parcel of socks and towels for them.

Geoffrey was sent to Warrington in mid-September to take over the 9th battalion, but found that it had not yet been formed! He took "a drunken rabble" of 420 men to join the 8th battalion to Seaford before returning to Tidworth for more training. At the end of September he heard from both his brothers - Roger becoming brigade major and Louis getting a commission as a temporary captain in the 11th Service Battalion of the Sherwood Foresters.

Geoffrey had bad news from Olive in early October that she had "overwrought herself" and he got leave to "try and help Olive and fix things up for her." When he got to Ashburton he found her "*much run down but bright and cheery as ever.*" He sent his son John with his nurse to his grandmother, Marian, in Cuddesdon and Geoffrey returned to Tidworth, where he dined with Roger. He visited John and his mother in early November when he found them very well, but it was not until later in the month that the family were all able to be together again.

In the middle of October the company was moved from barrack-rooms and tents to a new block of Jellalabad married quarters and Geoffrey was given a government cob to ride. As well as training, there were sporting fixtures between different companies, including rugby league matches – what Geoffrey calls "the Northern Union game".

The beginning of 1915 saw Geoffrey in hospital with influenza and laryngitis, followed by a few days at home with the family before rejoining the company at Winchester. Some platoons were comfortably billeted but others were in very indifferent places, with no sanitary arrangements, and they were found new billets. The whole town was "in an *indescribable* state of slush and mud". The training areas were not ideal - south east of Winchester consisted of open downs, but was spoilt by wire, while an attack staged for the benefit of the general in charge of Southern Command was a "most *miserable* show chiefly spoilt by being hampered by growing crops" with the farmer having to be compensated for damage caused!

Geoffrey was by now a major and the brigade was busy practising formations for the visit of the King who inspected the 13th Division on Chobham Ridges on 10 March. The following day Geoffrey took the future Labour Prime Minister, Captain Clement Attlee, who had also been posted to the 6th South Lancashire Regiment, to Cuddesdon to have tea with his stepmother, Marian.

In early April Geoffrey and Olive joined Roger and Helen in Bath and in May all four of them went to Lindfield to meet Louis' *fiancée*, Olive Slater. Louis and Olive's wedding took place at Bexhill on 1 June where "all went off splendidly". Marian, Roger and Helen, Geoffrey and Olive, Louis and aunt Sissie Coode all lunched together before the ceremony.

However, Geoffrey's battalion now received orders to fit drill clothing, which meant that they were bound for the Dardanelles; indeed embarkation for Gallipoli came within a fortnight of Louis' wedding. On the way to Alexandria they landed at Malta, where Geoffrey drove to the Braxia cemetery and saw his mother, Gertrude's, grave "beautifully kept with an oleander bush in full bloom". Geoffrey's interest in plants led him to look round the Noocha gardens in Alexandria which were "quite beautiful"; to appreciate the vineyards and pumpkins, when they reached Gallipoli and had to bivouac at Mudros; and, even when they went up the line and manned dugouts in Gully Ravine on dry and dusty slopes, he identified "a pale rose *Cistus*, a four-foot tree heath and a low growing variety of *Arbutus*".

Once when he took his company down to bathe, he came across Olive's brother, Joe, who had just come down from a ten-day spell in the trenches. The next day, 8 July, "he lunched with me and told me of the last scrap he was in when the Turks attacked half-heartedly and were driven back with severe casualties."

When the time came for Geoffrey's troops to move up the line, they found the trenches filthy with "flies and limbs protruding from the parapets". They then took over part of the fire trenches and the following day, 11 July, while the Dublin Fusiliers were attacking an enemy sap trench, Geoffrey shot his first Turk. He was enormous "I actually put him down as over seven feet! I just missed him with my first shot, but caught him in the right shoulder with my second. Most pluckily he kept up firing on the Dublins, until my third shot finished him off."

"Towards evening my young officers told me there was a man lying some 80 yards in front of our trench, whom they had been watching. One officer declared that he had seen him move, so I went to see for myself, and after some little time this man, who was lying on the burnt ground with a blackened face looking towards us, suddenly turned completely round facing the enemy, and I at once put an end to his little game, for he was evidently signalling to his own people."

The Welsh Fusiliers then took over these trenches and "we withdrew to the cliffs. I was glad enough of the rest as I had been troubled with gastroenteritis and some officers and several men had already gone sick with it." However, they soon had to move up to the front line again and were subject to fairly continuous shelling, but had few casualties.

After this they embarked and returned to Mudros to refit before recrossing to Gallipoli in a destroyer and disembarking at Anzac Cove. They then marched to their bivouac in Victoria Gully, where they suffered a few casualties from long-distance gunfire. Geoffrey wrote that "we reached the gully known as Chailak Dere" early in the morning of 7 August and, as we turned up it, "were met by a party of 100 Turkish prisoners being marched down. Our progress up the gully was slowed down by snipers." The next day they were given orders to entrench on an underfeature of Chunuk Bair, but "being severely sniped (with his second-in command being hit in the back) we withdrew to the beach and turned up Aghyll Dere and entrenched during darkness some 200 yards below the foot of Sari Bair".[42]

The heights of Sari Bair were the scene of Geoffrey's most distinctive contribution to the war, an assault where he showed both his

---

[42] National Army Museum 7709-22 – Account of Major G.R. Mott of the Battle of Sari Bair, presented by R.A. Savory. The quotations of Geoffrey's actions of 9/10 August are taken either from this account or from his memoirs.

individual skills and his qualities of leadership. The four day attempt to capture the heights (7-10 August) saw many battalions losing all their officers and in some cases almost all of their men killed or wounded. With shells screaming overhead, and bullets whistling around from the deadly fire of Turkish snipers, the morale of young untried soldiers was tested to the limit, as was the mettle of their officers.

On the morning of 9 August "I received orders from my commanding officer to attack Chunuk Bair in conjunction with the 1/6th Gurkhas who were on my right. The advance commenced at 4.30 a.m. and I only received half an hour's notice of it." The 1/6th Battalion Gurkha Rifles, under Major Allanson, had succeeded in establishing themselves 100 yards below the summit of Hill Q on the previous day and it was this force of the Gurkhas, aided by Geoffrey's detachment of the 6th South Lancashire Regiment, who succeeded in reaching the summit.

Geoffrey says that "as we left our trenches I noticed that that the Gurkha commander, Major Allanson, fell wounded and I thenceforward took command". In this precarious situation Geoffrey's ability to inspire his men, his distinctive use of the hunting horn and hunting cries and his exceptional shooting skills all came strongly into play. "When we were within 100 yards, the Turks vacated their first line of trenches which were weakly held" being quickly cleared by the British with their bayonets and the Gurkhas with their kukris. This charge against the Turks was "accompanied by view holloas and notes on my hunting horn" (which later came to be known as his Gallipoli horn).

They were by now "right over the top" of the summit. Allanson claimed later that they were driven back from the summit because they were shelled by the navy, but Geoffrey wrote that the appearance of a large number of Turkish reinforcements was the cause of the retreat as they "opened up a murderous fire with rifles and machine guns, completely enfilading us." He says that "we were in great danger of being surrounded, and consequently the only thing to do was to withdraw. This we did suffering very heavy casualties" to such an extent that "of the three companies in my command only two officers and myself came through unwounded. Personally I had a miraculous escape as my jacket was shot to pieces though I never received a wound." That evening he discovered that "my watch pocket had been shot through and my watch cut off the leather chain, also a small bottle of citronelle sent to me for flies, scattered to pieces."[43]

This force might have succeeded in holding their position on the summit if the other battalions, who were supposed to support the attack, had not been delayed by a combination of weak leadership, poor choice of route, wounded and dead men blocking their way and heavy machine-gun fire.[44] Geoffrey comments that "five new battalions, which should have cooperated on our right, never came up at all," while "the Warwicks, who should have been on my left, most unfortunately did not receive their orders in time, and so we were left with our left flank in the air!" Geoffrey always regretted that the assault had been a failure and wrote many years later that, had the other battalions "come up in support as they should have done, I am convinced that this important but disappointing campaign would have been a complete success."[45]

As it was, the Turks under Mustafa Kemal counter-attacked successfully the next morning, 10 August, and by the end of the day the fight for the Sari Bair heights was over. Geoffrey's own experiences that day started at dawn when "as rations were being issued, enemy machine guns poured a terrific fire on us" causing many casualties. He collected 40 or 50 men and "led them up a steep wooded knoll called Gurkha Post, on the top of which was a shallow trench, which proved to be nothing but a death trap, and I at once had it cleared and kept my men under cover on the reverse slope."

Geoffrey had always specialized in musketry training and he now found himself in a position where he was able to use his skills as a marksman to inflict considerable damage on the enemy. "Keeping clear of the trench, I crawled to a spot where the fallen bough of a tree would conceal me from view, and here I fired continuously for over four hours".

During this Turkish counter-attack "I had many a good target in the open", but much of his firing was against those Turks who "rolled

---

[43] P. Liddle *Men of Gallipoli* (London, 1976) p. 208

[44] T. Travers *Gallipoli 1915* (London, 2001) p. 131-3 provides an analysis of the reasons for the failure to hold the summit. However, he mistakes Geoffrey's account of Sari Bair in the National Army Museum - 7709-22 – as being that of R.A. Savory. There is no doubt that this is the account written by Geoffrey (this is also stated in the Museum's Card Index).

[45] Military historians remain divided about this but agree that there was a chance of success if all their forces had been deployed.

down the slopes of Sari Bair, some 800 yards away" taking cover behind small green bushes. "When about a dozen had collected behind a bush, I would put five rounds rapid fire into it. Fresh rifles were passed up to me as the barrels became too heated, and, of course, I was kept well supplied with ammunition. An NCO on the slope behind me kept a tally of my 'certainties'. These, of course, only included those I could clearly identify, for it was impossible to be sure of results when firing into a group concealed by a bush." Geoffrey says that "my easiest target" was a machine gun team 350 yards away and "I completely wiped out the whole team". In total, although "*definite certainties* only numbered 47, the actual 'bag' could well have been more than double that number. Quite a few must have been hit behind those small bushes, for few were seen to emerge from them." "Members of his company said that his aim was so good that it was not necessary for anybody else to join him on the firing line." [46]

After all this action, when Geoffrey heard that "units on my right and left had all retired, I decided it was time to leave the knoll, and so we dropped back by 'Dead Man's Gully' which was literally strewn with dead and wounded." During the withdrawal "there was one short stretch which was under continuous rifle fire" and "we were fortunate to get back to the battalion with few casualties."

"After seeing the men comfortably settled and fed, I went to report to brigade HQ. General Cayley said in a severe tone "I am not going to listen to a word you say until you have had something to eat!" However, when he made his report, General Cayley "listened most attentively and, thanking me, said 'I am going to recommend you for a DSO'." Nevertheless, because the campaign was a failure, Geoffrey says that a DSO "never came my way but only a mention in despatches".[47]

At the end of the month Roger, having heard from Geoffrey about his actions against the Turks, wrote to Olive. "Many congratulations: you must be as proud of old Geoff as a hen with three legs! Well done, he! It was a splendid description of a fight – what topping letters he does write. I was so 'bucked' when I read it that I've been reading extracts to everyone I have met this morning! Can't

---

[46] J. Laffin *'Damn the Dardanelles' The Agony of Gallipoli* (London, 1980) p. 123
[47] *London Gazette* 28 January 1916

you just see him, yelling tally-ho! and blowing (his hunting horn) 'fit to bust', Whoowhooping [48] and all the rest of it? He is wonderfully lucky to have got through unscathed and must bear a charmed life. I do hope he will get a really nice honour out of it. I can't get over his bagging 47 Turks on his own!"

Geoffrey was indeed lucky to have survived. Besides the commanding officer and himself only four officers came through unscathed, the rest were either killed or wounded. By the next day, 11 August, the commanding officer had gone sick and Geoffrey took over command of the battalion and also, temporarily, of the 9th Warwicks who had no officers left until an officer took control the following day. By then "we were just under 200 strong and the Warwicks 250."

A few days later he received a consignment of eggs and bread, which he distributed among those men who had been engaged in the recent fighting, and they were relieved by the Connaughts and were able to go into rest bivouacs. Geoffrey's gastroenteritis was, meanwhile, getting worse and he was given a "most hospitable dugout" and arrowroot. Food presents from home also kept on arriving "and most welcome they were".

However, despite having a bad time with gastroenteritis and fever, Geoffrey stayed at his post in his dugout. The medical officer tried to persuade him to go sick, but he refused to do so until a regular officer could take over. He had to ask for volunteers for sniping and reconnaissance work and was "greatly relieved" to discover "some stout-hearted fellows out of the latest draft" one of whom "a great bearded lad, was a South African war veteran of my A company. He had given up a profitable fruiterers business to join up."

On 27 August the adjutant of the 6th Loyal North Lancs took over the battalion and "assisted by my soldier servant (Private Ryan), I managed to get to the 39th Field Ambulance, and eventually was carried on a stretcher to the good ship *Maheno* a New Zealand boat, fitted and staffed entirely by people of that colony. This was the first shipload of casualties she had taken aboard. I believe she could have taken over 500, and fear that she got them that night as a bloody battle began to rage, and Ryan and I had quite a number of 'overs' to dodge on our way down."

---

[48] A hunting cry when the otter or fox has been caught.

Two days later Geoffrey was transferred to a temporary hospital ship "very dirty and not fitted up as a hospital ship and terribly understaffed" where he received little attention. But, despite the tummy, a sore throat and Gallipoli sores, the sea was calm and they reached Gibraltar on 6 September where the medical officer refused to let him go ashore. But the first officer looked up Humphry Hill (Marian's brother) "who came aboard in the evening brought me books and papers and gave me all the family news". On 15 September the ship was picked up by two destroyers in foggy weather and escorted into Plymouth Sound and Devonport Dockyard.

CHAPTER ELEVEN

THE FIRST WORLD WAR - 1915-1918

When Geoffrey returned to Devonport in September 1915 he wrote "I shall *never* forget the delightful feeling of being in England (and Devon) once again". He went before a medical board and was recommended for two month's sick leave, while the doctor cleaned and dressed his 'peninsula sore' on his left hand, after which Olive took him home. "The pleasure of being with the little family was almost too much for me." A few days later they took the train to Totnes, on by steamboat to Dartmouth, then by train to Paignton "where we paddled and went to a picture show" and then, after tea, took a motor bus to Totnes and home by train. What a contrast to recent events in Gallipoli and the only problem was John being sick on the sands!

Geoffrey also lost no time going hunting again and looking up old friends and his stepmother, Marian, came to stay for a few days. But the effects of war were also evident – one friend Gibb was blind in both eyes from his wounds in Flanders and Geoffrey had to describe his own dogs to him. He also had to talk a lot about Gallipoli to a family whose two sons had fallen there.

Geoffrey and Olive left the children with Olive's parents before travelling to Limehurst where they saw Helen and the family and onto Cuddesdon to see his stepmother, Marian, who took them to call on the Bishop of Oxford at the Palace. They then went to London to see *Quinney's* at the Haymarket and dined at Les Gobbelins with his cousin C.C. Mott, before going on to The Empire.[49]

Another medical board in November recommended another month's leave and the doctor lanced a septic sore near his left groin for the next few days. But sick leave ended just after Christmas and "the beginning of another phase in this world war as far as I am concerned". The contrast was brought home to him immediately

---

[49] See Mott family tree p. 162

when he experienced a very cold night in his new quarters, a wooden hut, "in spite of seven thicknesses of blanket!!"

He was attached temporarily to the 6th Battalion, South Lancashire Regiment, which he found rather tedious and monotonous, but he looked up friends and relations whenever possible, including Arthur Mott and Maud at Whitton Hall and Richard Hill and Emily and their children Doreen and Humphry, who was later to marry Roger's daughter Sylvia.[50] He also met a Major Lumb who knew his father at Aldershot in 1877.

However, by the end of February 1916 sciatica began to get a hold again, not helped by continuous snow and frost. When he saw Sir James Barr he "found him very charming and he refused to charge me any fee! He says my muscles have wasted and I should have six weeks at least *absolute rest*." He was granted sick leave and was able to return to Devon and the family.

He heard from the regiment that the authorities proposed sending him to Bath for treatment and, after attending a medical board, he was recommended for another three month's sick leave and was admitted to the Red Cross Officers' convalescent home in Bath for three and a half weeks where Mrs Colhoun, the matron, turned out to be an old friend of the Parlbys. The doctor prescribed massage, which took place before breakfast, and this enabled him to go out to the Bath and County Club and to go on a number of expeditions to Castle Combe a "beautiful old village, quite unspoilt", and to Bristol Zoo, where there were "no otters!" He also took Mrs Colhoun to the Theatre Royal, Bath, but when he motored in a superb Rolls Royce with Captain Cheales to tea one day, a Dr Melsome came in afterwards "and prescribed for me!!" On their return to the home "Mrs Colhoun did not *at all* approve of this!" and relations were "*somewhat strained*!!"

While at Bath he learnt that he had been transferred to the 'second reserve' and, when he left the home at the beginning of July, he was able to return to Devon and take the family to Dawlish for three weeks, as he was granted another two month's sick leave. It was not until 24 October that he was able to persuade the medical board that he was fit enough for general service abroad, though the president "expressed a doubt as to my being able to remain there for two weeks!"

---

[50] See Mott and Hill family trees pp. 162, 168

But in mid-November he rejoined the regiment at Press Heath, after an absence of seven months, where most of the time was taken up with route-marches, and bombing practice. With troops constantly coming and going, by mid-December his company consisted of "two officers and 26 other ranks!" but 137 recruits arrived and joined that evening.

At the beginning of December aunt Alice wrote and wired that his stepmother, Marian, was to be operated on that day. He went down by rail the next day and dined with aunt Alice but, when he saw his stepmother, he was "greatly shocked with her appearance". However the following day she was comfortable after a good night's rest and he had to return to the regiment. At the beginning of January 1917 he heard again from aunt Alice that her youngest sister, Maude, had died a few days earlier. By then Roger was home on leave and Geoffrey received a wire to join him in Oxford the following week. This he did and he and Olive dined with Roger and Helen and then went on to Wyndham's Theatre. The following day Geoffrey and Olive went to Oxford and went straight to St John's Home to see his stepmother who was "fearfully weak and exhausted." Roger and Helen arrived in Oxford in the evening and stayed at Magdalen College with the president. Geoffrey had to say farewell to his stepmother and aunt Alice, Roger and Helen and return to barracks, but less than a week later had a wire from aunt Alice to say that his stepmother "passed away in her sleep at three this morning". Geoffrey returned to Oxford where his two brothers were also staying, Louis having come up from Waddesdon in Buckinghamshire, where he was now curate, after leaving the army. At the funeral the Bishop of Oxford read the lesson and her brother Richard and her sisters Alice and Louise were among the mourners.

Roger was home on leave because when he wrote to Olive about Geoffrey's exploits in Gallipoli at end of August 1915, he said "we are off in quite a few days' time – France I believe". They were billeted in villages west of Amiens before moving to Cachy, and going into the line for instruction. "I remember going round the trenches beyond Villers-Brettonneux, where we had to go quietly, because the Hun trenches were only about 20 yards away. But for some reason we never took over those trenches, but were moved about, to Corbie, Villers-Bocage and Mollins-aux-Bois – where brigade headquarters were in a very nice chateau. At one place we were inspected by the corps commander, who proved to be General C.C. Munro of the 'Queen's'. He told Brigadier-General Poole that he had known me as a small boy, and had me put across his knee and smacked me – suiting the action to the word, to the amusement of the bystanders!" As Colonel Munro he had met Geoffrey and told him the same story when he was on his first musketry course at Hythe.

But having just taken over trenches near Albert, orders were received to move to Macedonia. "What a lovely place Salonika looked, as we steamed up the long bay! At close quarters it was not nearly so attractive. Conditions were rather tricky when we disembarked – a Greek army still in being, somewhere between us and the Bulgars, and we did not know what their reactions might be. The division settled down on the plain, a little to the north of Salonika and I remember our anxiety as a large Greek force marched by, close to us, in thick fog. However, as more troops arrived, we were able to persuade the Greeks to withdraw their forces. Then, heavy snow fell and we were uncomfortable in our tents until we had dug the inside well down. And one day, the thick weather cleared and we could see the country for miles, even as far as the Albanian hills, 100 miles away."

"The men were employed for several weeks, digging a trench-line near Largaza – which we called 'The Birdcage', which we eventually occupied. We lived fairly well, as Salonika was well-supplied, and trips to the town with good meals at Flora's or the French Club at *Tour Blanche*, were popular. The Bulgars were miles away to the north, and in those early days we never saw a hostile plane."

Eventually they received orders to move and take over the trench-line from the French facing Doiran. These trenches "were wretched. My opposite number produced a lovely plan of them, but when we went round with him we failed to find a good many and discovered that the plan was mostly 'wishful thinking'! It meant a lot of hard digging for the troops, mostly in rocky soil. Whilst up there, a day came when we saw, for the first time 24 planes flying in formation. This was the first appearance of what came to be called 'Richtofen's Circus'. It was on its way to bomb Salonika."

The First Battle of Doiran took place on the night of 26/27 April 1917. Brigadier-General Poole "hoped it would be carried out in daylight, but that was not to be. The brigade had to attack just to the west of the lake, as far as a rocky hill called '*Petit Couronne*'. (We took over the names of several localities from the French, and I named others after places we had known during our training in England 'Wylye Ravine', 'Silbury Hill' and so on)."

"The advance took place over a steep valley, rock-strewn, and well-registered by enemy artillery. Here the brigade suffered most of its casualties. Officers who had undergone shelling in France said this was much worse, on account of the noise of shells bursting in so confined a space, and hitting rocks instead of soft ground." The Devon and Wilts troops, caught in the ravine, were "killed at long distance by the heavy shells of German naval guns, always hellish when used on land".

Roger says that "the 7th Wilts – by now a splendid, well-disciplined and smart battalion, did very well, and got into the Bulgar trenches; and some of the 10th Devons captured 'Petit Couronne', but the casualties were very severe, and the troops were ordered to return to their trenches. We had acted as a brigade group, with Royal Artillery, Royal Engineers, machine gun corps and trench mortar men attached for the battle – and we had no less than 76 officer casualties in the group. The poor old Devons and Wilts suffered very heavily, in spite of their gallantry. There was an armistice next day to bring in the wounded and bury the dead" as the Bulgarians allowed British stretcher bearers to collect the wounded from the ravine.

"Twice more the Doiran position was attacked; the first time, a whole division was put in to attack what had been our brigade objective; and later two divisions, when the last battle took place. The former failed, as we had, and the latter only got through after a terrific battle, in which one battalion came out with one wounded officer and about 20 men! So we had been given an impossible task, and were so knocked about that we were pulled out and sent to a nice quiet sector east of Doiran, on the Krusha Balkan hills. Brigade headquarters were in a nice little village called Karamudli. Here we stayed for some time, until we were shifted to just east of the Vardar."

To make things worse, throughout the course of this campaign "Macedonia was a most unhealthy place, and malaria attacked nearly everybody – a virulent form of it. One night, a whole battalion in, I think, the 28th division, was struck down, only the transport, which was on higher ground, escaping. Many men died in the ambulances before they could reach hospital." In total British forces suffered 162, 517 cases of the disease.

But for Roger "hardly had the brigade reached the Vardar trenches than a wire arrived saying that I had been promoted to DAAG (Deputy Assistant Adjutant General) of the 27th division. That division was on the Sturma front with headquarters at Dimitric, and thither I went with Hitchman, my batman, Poultney, my groom, and two horses, for I had been issued with a second charger, and got a nice little bay, which I called Karamudli, from George Dowell, my old friend of Wall days, who was director of remounts at Salonika."

"There was very little fighting on the Sturma front, but the office work was terrific; so much so that I rarely got the chance of a ride, or any exercise. In addition to the normal 'A' work I had to organize entertainment for the troops. We got a clever fellow to run a pantomime, fixed up a concert-party, and a cinema show. In the summer we had a wonderful horse show, near Dzuma-Mah, a village on high ground, to which we moved for the hot weather, to get away from the malarial Sturma region."

Roger was mentioned in despatches in December 1916, was commended for his gallant conduct and distinguished service in Salonika in October 1917 and was awarded the Military Cross for his service there in June 1918. That service had ended after "long hours in the office and no exercise" resulted in him getting "rather badly run-down" with the effect that he "had the worst lumbago attack I've ever had, which meant a fortnight in hospital". After this "when exchanges were arranged with 'opposite numbers' who had never left England, I was sent home, and became DAAG of the 69th division, with its headquarters at Retford", where he was able to take an empty house, furnish it with the minimum requirements, and move the family there. Later the division moved to Clipstone, and he took the family to Pleasley, where they stayed until the war ended.

In March 1917 Geoffrey had told the inspecting General Alderson, that he wanted to get out to the front again and he told him that he had recommended him for a command of a battalion at the Front. But nothing happened until two months later and the visit of the commanding officer of the Western Command, General Pitcairn-Campbell. General Campbell had commanded the division when Geoffrey had been at the Curragh before the war and Geoffrey, knowing his love of ceremonial parades, had suggested to his commanding officer that they should organize one for him. He hesitated, saying that it could not be shown on the war programme, "however,

117

when I assured him not only that it need not appear on it, but that I would train our splendid youngsters in ceremonial myself in the early mornings each day until the inspection, he agreed."

"Everything went off superbly" and the general was loud in his praises. When Geoffrey sat on his left at lunch after the parade Colonel Wanless said to him "You know Major Mott, general?" "Yes indeed" was his reply "we're very old friends" which somewhat surprised me, though he evidently remembered me at the Curragh, and he talked to me throughout the meal of the good old days in Ireland." So when Geoffrey pointed out that, when an application was put in to transfer to a fighting unit in France the CO would invariably tear it up, he said "that will be alright my boy." It was 'alright' because less than a month later he received his orders to proceed to the Front and sailed for France.

Geoffrey joined his regiment in billets on the outskirts of Ypres and soon found himself in the front line. During the Passchendaele fighting "I was on three occasions buried when a shell burst close to me. On the first two of these I was fortunately able to extricate myself, but the third time had to be dug out." Like all soldiers he had to endure the mud and water of the trenches, but, as he puts it, "it would be tedious to dwell on the numerous periods in the trenches and the hardships which all had to endure."

What comes across is his ability to enjoy things as well. Before setting out for France he had been given a new charger, Polly, a nice chestnut mare. When he took the battalion out for field-firing practice, accompanied by an enormous village dog, "suddenly a fox crossed the road, little more than 50 yards in front of me, and off went the excited dog madly in pursuit. Handing over to my second in command, I speedily followed, and after a short gallop *reynard* eluded further pursuit by slipping into a badger sett. Never shall I forget the scene, for surrounding the holes and the white chalky heaps thrown up outside them, was a large colony of lovely mauve pasque-flower – *anemone pulsatilla*. The area covered by these I reckon could not have been less than half an acre. A truly wonderful sight!"

And on another occasion, when they were billeted in a small town and he was not satisfied with his billet, "I went to the mayor who most kindly placed his comfortable house at my disposal, and I was well looked after by his charming daughter, who turned out to be a keen sportswoman."

The next period of heavy fighting came at the end of May 1918,

'Trucklepark'. The setting and the garden clearly gave them great pleasure and in November Geoffrey started planting an apple orchard with 18 trees.

When Geoffrey was once asked whether he was interested in gardens, he replied that it was his keenest hobby next to hunting. In1932 he met the Reverend W. Keble-Martin, the great botanist, and went on more than one expedition with him in search of wild flowers. The following year he went to "see some of his wonderful wild flower pictures" and "I took him a fine specimen of *archangelica* from my wild garden".

He carried out a lot of planting work in his Lustleigh garden including an area dedicated to azaleas and rhododendrons, heaths and *ericas* such as *lusitanica, veietchii*, vegans and Irish heaths and various shrubs including, *cotoneaster frigida* and *salisfolia, viburnum birkwoodii, veronicas* and *deutzia veitchi*. When visiting a garden at Lymington in the New Forest "a real gem caught our eye, which the head gardener told me was *cornus florida rubra*. I ordered one of these later, and it thrived and was much admired in my Lustleigh garden."

An important part of Roger, Geoffrey and Louis' lives came to an end in the inter-war years, that of Manadon. It came about because their uncle - their mother Gertrude's brother, Reginald Parlby - died there in January 1923, having "succumbed to pneumonia". Two weeks before his death Reginald made his last public appearance in Plymouth when he helped his wife to distribute presents from the Christmas tree to, in the words of the Plymouth Mercury "the little inmates" of the Devon and Cornwall female orphanage. He was only ill for a week but "despite the best medical skill he did not recover". Roger and Geoffrey were both present at the funeral which once again took place at "the picturesque little church of Pennycross situated in a corner of the Manadon estate" and their brother Louis, vicar of Hennock, near Bovey Tracey, assisted at the service. A few months later a service was held at Holy Trinity Church, Crown Hill, where the Bishop of Plymouth dedicated a memorial window to their late uncle.

Reginald's widow Violet remained at Manadon for some years and Geoffrey went to stay there at the end of 1925 with Olive when they saw Violet's daughters, Blanche and Cynthia, act in a production at the Royal Marine Theatre, Plymouth. They spent another "delightful weekend" with their Parlby relatives at Manadon in January 1928 and Reginald's younger brother, Walter, came home from Canada in early April, which was the first time he had been in England since 1910 when Geoffrey had seen him and his wife off from Liverpool on the *Virginian*. They saw a lot of him at Manadon over the next few months which brought back memories of the time when, being up at Oxford, he had brought several of his St John's College friends for an archery meeting and had taken over the arch-room where they could make as much noise as they liked. This was obviously typical of his time at Oxford because "he had been sent down for indulging too much in sport, and laid low for the rest of the term at his brother-in-law's place at Parke, Bovey Tracey where he had as much hunting as he wanted."

In 1935 Geoffrey planted a *eucryphia cordiflora*, which he had been given by his aunt Violet from Manadon, in his garden at Lustleigh. But by then Roger and Geoffrey's cousin Cecil Parlby, who had inherited Manadon after his father's death, had married "a young Scots girl who was not interested in Devon" and he now sold Manadon to a syndicate. Later the admiralty purchased 100 acres of the estate, and Manadon became a Royal Engineering College, HMS *Thunderer*.

Geoffrey wrote that 9 April 1936 "was one of the saddest days of my life. After having lunch with my aunt Violet and cousins Cynthia and John, I took many photographs of lovely old Manadon." For Roger the decision was equally poignant. He wrote that the estate "is being built over; the old house is not being pulled down, but I feel that I never want to see it again, preferring that it should remain in my memory as a dream-house, remembered and beloved."

The following January, Reeves, who had served the Parlby family so well as butler for no less than 46 years and had been renowned as a wonderful ventriloquist who could make voices come out of anywhere, died. The funeral service was taken by Louis, who was by now vicar of Chudleigh Knighton.[51] Reeves' final employer, aunt Violet Parlby, had moved to the old vicarage at Bishop's Lydeard, near Taunton.

Another long-lasting connection was ended with the death of Charles Mott's last surviving sister, aunt Sissie Coode, in 1926. Her husband Arthur, who had been a prominent banker and magistrate in

---

[51] He was vicar there from 1924 until 1950.

St Austell, and had come to Charles' aid by helping him to avoid having to return to India, had died in 1910. Much of her estate went to Roger, Geoffrey and Louis together with her niece Elma, the daughter of her sister Henrietta.[52]

By now both Roger and Geoffrey were becoming well-known in their local communities, and both put on pantomimes at Christmas 1922. Roger inherited his father Charles' love of acting and writing verses and his grandmother Louise's love of music, and the pantomime that he wrote brings out his talents as a writer, composer of songs and verses and as an organizer. The travelling pantomime put on by the Quantock Pantomime Company was called *Robinson Crusoe*. In true pantomime style the action throughout was influenced by a villain 'The Terrible Toad' (played by Roger and Helen's son, Charles) and a heroine 'The Fairy Good Luck' (played by his sister Sylvia). The action started with hunt followers listening to the progress of the hunt before passengers such as Sir Crowcombe Heathfield, a millionaire, his wife (played by Helen) and their daughter Zoggs, Mrs Crusoe and her lively son Robinson, (played by Roger), and other Quantock characters arrived to catch a bus travelling to Watchet. When the bus driver finally turned up he told Sir Crowcombe "bus broken down at the bottom of the hill". So while the puncture was mended the passengers had a competition to compose the best limerick based on local villages, one example being:

There was a young man of Bicknoller,
Who wore an absurdly high collar;
He paid for his pride for he very soon died,
He was simply unable to swallow!

The party then went to the local inn where they discovered that only 'soft drinks' could be served because of prohibition. But the landlord explained that, as in America, "the more they stop the drink, the more they drink!" "We have a chemist's shop attached to every public house" and with the help of the inn's "chemistry department" various 'tonics' were produced on mine host's prescription. The problem of transport was then solved by the timely appearance of 'Ida the Glider', who undertook to convey the party to Watchet by glider, but on the way Ida lost control of the machine and they had to lighten

---

[52] See Mott family tree p. 162

the load by throwing people out. All the passengers found themselves on a desert island, where Robinson met Man Friday, donned
the garb of a true Robinson Crusoe and declared his love for Sir
Crowcombe's daughter, Zoggs. Under Robinson's guidance the party
descended by special submarine to the bottom of the sea where, by
the good offices of the Old Man of the Sea, they were transported
back to the mainland, finally coming ashore near Doniford. The convenient presence of a travelling circus enabled them to fit themselves out with dry, if rather fanciful, clothes, with Lady Crowcombe
dressed as Queen Elizabeth and Lydia, a milkmaid, as 'The Spirit of
Jazz' in a 1920's outfit. The party ended up safely back in a cosy inn
with Robinson about to marry Zoggs.

The cast also performed songs with catchy tunes such as 'a little
drop o' cider and a bit o' bread and cheese' which according to the
Somerset County Gazette "added considerably to the brightness of
the production".

The other day I had such a rotten bit o' luck,
I thought I'd backed a winner, but oh, it came unstuck.
I felt so very wretched, and all was looking black
Until a jolly fellow, he clapped me on the back
And he murmured –

Chorus
What about a little drop of cider, William?
Just one little drop, do.
A little drop o' cider and a bit o' bread and cheese,
That's the stuff to put you at your ease.
Cheer up; why be so depressed
Don't make a hullabaloo!
What about a little drop of cider William
Just one little drop, do!

I loved a lovely maiden and asked her to be mine;
She thanked me very kindly but said she must decline.
So as the job was hopeless and I was feeling blue
I ran and told my mother and asked her what to do
And she murmured -

Chorus
What about a little drop of cider, William?
Just one little drop, do.
A little drop o' cider and a bit o' bread and cheese,
That's the stuff to put you at your ease.
Cheer up; why be so depressed
Don't make a hullabaloo!
What about a little drop of cider William
Just one little drop, do!

I took a little joy-ride upon a motor bike
And seated on the pillion a girl I rather like.
We crashed into a lamp-post, and I was nearly dead;
The girl she sat beside me a-stroking of my head.
And she whispered -

Chorus
What about a little drop of cider, William?
Just one little drop, do.
A little drop o' cider and a bit o' bread and cheese,
That's the stuff to put you at your ease.
Cheer up; why be so depressed
Don't make a hullabaloo!
What about a little drop of cider William
Just one little drop, do!

Roger remembers that "we performed at various villages and had a lot of fun. A lorry used to move our gear, scenery, piano, electric lighting, plant and dresses." He writes that "I shall not forget a tough journey from Stogumber to Handy Cross in the snow, and what a job it was getting up the hill from Stogumber. I walking behind with a vast stone, and putting it under a rear-wheel every few yards when the lorry skidded!"

Geoffrey wrote that Roger's pantomime was "of a far higher quality than mine", but he also wrote a "kind of pantomime which I called 'Tally-ho – a Fantasy in Three Acts'." But it "was great fun. Names of local sporting celebrities were introduced" as well as "well-known places on and around the moor". His brother Louis and his elder son John were among the cast.

Roger's pantomime was revived at Christmas in 1925 and 1928, with a few changes from the original production, and Geoffrey went to see it at King's College, Taunton in January 1929, at the end of a run where it had been performed at seven venues and had to be adapted to seven different stages. The Somerset County Gazette said of the final night at King's College that "the clever author and his supporters deserve the heartiest congratulations" for "three hours of rollicking fun without a dull moment".

With all three brothers living in the West Country their paths crossed quite frequently as they stayed with each other and went out hunting. In April 1928 the three brothers and their families spent a day together, lunching at Haldon and having tea on Dawlish beach.[53] Two years later, in January 1930, gales damaged the sea walls at Dawlish so seriously that trains had to be diverted on to the Southern line. There was a hole in the wall big enough to take two locomotives. This coincided with Geoffrey and Olive's silver wedding anniversary which they celebrated with Olive's parents at Ivybridge over a saddle of mutton. Roger gave Geoffrey a silver fox ashtray.

Roger and Helen "lived for 14 years in the lovely Quantock country, which we got to know intimately and loved – an unspoilt piece of England and full of friendly people." On Tuesdays the local Taunton store sent someone out to Bagborough to discuss the week's deliveries with Helen and then, having agreed the order, it was put together and delivered on Fridays. Roger became keen on folk-dancing and eventually became the honorary secretary of the Somerset branch of the English Folk Dance society, while his dramatic interests continued in June 1928 when he was involved in the Taunton Pageant. This was organized by the Master of the Pageant, Major M.F. Cely-Trevilian who "put up a wonderful show". Roger "was cast for the part of Colonel Kirke, and commanded a detachment of 'Kirke's lambs'. These were a lot of old soldiers, who were irreverently called the 'Bar-lambs'!" This part of the pageant was set at the time of Judge Jefferies' Assizes and prisoners were erecting scarlet draperies of the court under the direction of 'Kirke's lambs'. Colonel Kirke found Jefferies "too bloody-minded for me" with the result that "there are times when it irks me to do his bidding". He

---

[53] Louis and Olive had by now a third daughter, Suzanne, born in 1923.

was not averse to a bit of commission on the side as "a man must put by a little for his old age" and agreed that he could arrange the escape of poorer prisoners for £20 a piece if enough of them "broke out".

Roger also became very interested in genealogy in these years and carried out a vast amount of research into the family trees of a number of branches of the Mott family and families connected with them such as the Kynastons, Oakeleys, Parlbys, Radcliffes, Hills, Cumberleges and Fenwicks. In 1934 he also wrote notes on different members of the Mott family using the family papers that he possessed. As well as this his inheritance of Spring Grove in Kent led him into an interest in the Boys and Brett families and, as well as compiling family trees, he acquired the contents of an old muniment chest containing deeds and a few letters of Dr Thomas Brett, the well-known non-juror, which he sold to the Bodleian Library in Oxford in 1933.

It was the consequences of another will that led Roger and Helen to yet another move in April 1933, this time to the New Forest. This came about because of Allum Green, a house a little way out of Lyndhurst, which had been "bought and enlarged by Mr George Fenwick, Nell's grandfather". Helen later wrote a memoir called *The Fenwick Saga* in which she remembers that Allum Green "to start with, was a cottage residence with a few fields, but though more or less keeping the 'cottagey' look, (her grandfather) built on a lot of extra rooms. He made an enormous kitchen garden with a high red-brick wall surrounding it, also built three cottages, one nice enough to lend to friends, the other for the gardener and farmer. A small Guernsey herd provided lovely cream and butter, and there were pigs and poultry. The family would go to Allum Green when the London season was over, and remain there until the end of October or early November, and they loved it."

Allum Green "was left to aunt Sophy by grandpapa, who died in 1913, and she lived there in great contentment till her own death, 18 October 1932." Aunt Sophy left it between Helen and two of her cousins. None of them wanted to live there, but they did not want it to go out of the family, so Helen bought them out. The result was that Roger and Helen "sold the house at Bagborough, keeping some of the land, and moved into Allum Green on 26 April 1933, just in time to celebrate our silver wedding there. As usual, we made certain alterations to the house, and installed oil-heating – which occasionally gave me a lot of trouble! We took over three servants, Wilding, the chauffeur; Broomfield, the gardener, and a garden boy. The lovely walled-garden was a great attraction, with its fruit, and a beautiful pair of iron gates."

While at Allum Green, "one of the great days was when Sylvia announced her engagement to my godson, Humphry Hill." Humphry was the son of Richard Hill, who was the brother of Roger and Geoffrey's stepmother, Marian, and thus continued the Hill family connection.[54] Richard Hill had been adjutant of the Royal Irish Constabulary and Chief Constable of Cornwall. Humphry and Sylvia's wedding took place at Lyndhurst in March 1936. Another attachment that developed while they lived at Allum Green, was between Roger and Helen's youngest son David, who went to the Royal Naval College, Dartmouth, and Sheila Prentice, whom he was later to marry.

---

[54] See Hill family tree p. 168

St Austell, and had come to Charles' aid by helping him to avoid having to return to India, had died in 1910. Much of her estate went to Roger, Geoffrey and Louis together with her niece Elma, the daughter of her sister Henrietta.[52]

By now both Roger and Geoffrey were becoming well-known in their local communities, and both put on pantomimes at Christmas 1922. Roger inherited his father Charles' love of acting and writing verses and his grandmother Louise's love of music, and the pantomime that he wrote brings out his talents as a writer, composer of songs and verses and as an organizer. The travelling pantomime put on by the Quantock Pantomime Company was called *Robinson Crusoe*. In true pantomime style the action throughout was influenced by a villain 'The Terrible Toad' (played by Roger and Helen's son, Charles) and a heroine 'The Fairy Good Luck' (played by his sister Sylvia). The action started with hunt followers listening to the progress of the hunt before passengers such as Sir Crowcombe Heathfield, a millionaire, his wife (played by Helen) and their daughter Zoggs, Mrs Crusoe and her lively son Robinson, (played by Roger), and other Quantock characters arrived to catch a bus travelling to Watchet. When the bus driver finally turned up he told Sir Crowcombe "bus broken down at the bottom of the hill". So while the puncture was mended the passengers had a competition to compose the best limerick based on local villages, one example being:

There was a young man of Bicknoller,
Who wore an absurdly high collar;
He paid for his pride for he very soon died,
He was simply unable to swallow!

The party then went to the local inn where they discovered that only 'soft drinks' could be served because of prohibition. But the landlord explained that, as in America, "the more they stop the drink, the more they drink!" "We have a chemist's shop attached to every public house" and with the help of the inn's "chemistry department" various 'tonics' were produced on mine host's prescription. The problem of transport was then solved by the timely appearance of 'Ida the Glider', who undertook to convey the party to Watchet by glider, but on the way Ida lost control of the machine and they had to lighten

---

[52] See Mott family tree p. 162

the load by throwing people out. All the passengers found themselves on a desert island, where Robinson met Man Friday, donned the garb of a true Robinson Crusoe and declared his love for Sir Crowcombe's daughter, Zoggs. Under Robinson's guidance the party descended by special submarine to the bottom of the sea where, by the good offices of the Old Man of the Sea, they were transported back to the mainland, finally coming ashore near Doniford. The convenient presence of a travelling circus enabled them to fit themselves out with dry, if rather fanciful, clothes, with Lady Crowcombe dressed as Queen Elizabeth and Lydia, a milkmaid, as 'The Spirit of Jazz' in a 1920's outfit. The party ended up safely back in a cosy inn with Robinson about to marry Zoggs.

The cast also performed songs with catchy tunes such as 'a little drop o' cider and a bit o' bread and cheese' which according to the Somerset County Gazette "added considerably to the brightness of the production".

The other day I had such a rotten bit o' luck,
I thought I'd backed a winner, but oh, it came unstuck.
I felt so very wretched, and all was looking black
Until a jolly fellow, he clapped me on the back
And he murmured –

Chorus
What about a little drop of cider, William?
Just one little drop, do.
A little drop o' cider and a bit o' bread and cheese,
That's the stuff to put you at your ease.
Cheer up; why be so depressed
Don't make a hullabaloo!
What about a little drop of cider William
Just one little drop, do!

I loved a lovely maiden and asked her to be mine;
She thanked me very kindly but said she must decline.
So as the job was hopeless and I was feeling blue
I ran and told my mother and asked her what to do
And she murmured -

with the Second Battle of the Aisne, which involved tremendous losses. On one day the "Boche attacked in the early morning and got through on our immediate left. Owing to shelling we withdrew to Magneux. We were shelled and machine gunned out of that to Crugny arriving there about 9 p.m." He described it as a "trying day" with enemy planes "very active and ours not on the spot". This was followed by "hasty orders to take up a front of nearly five miles with 200 men".

A few days later he received orders to form a composite battalion of 500, which became known officially as 'Mott's Force'. They were expected to march 30 kilometres "which I realized was quite impossible in view of the short time allotted, and the poor condition of the men. This I pointed out to the camp commandant and suggested that he should phone the division and ask for lorries to convey us. As he hesitated, I pressed him to do this, telling him that he was well in with the Divisional Commander. I added 'you never know what you can do until you try'. When the reply came it was a disappointing one. But I told him that I had studied my map carefully and found there was an ideal spot only 15 kilometres away, and suggested marching there, and after a bathe in the river and a hot meal, that lorries could meet us there and take us on to our destination, so that the men could go into the line more or less 'fighting fit'. This time they agreed to co-operate and all went well."

They came under bombardment with a sprinkling of mustard gas for six or seven hours a day over the next few days, and Geoffrey "had a painful and very trying time, nearly suffocating" after which he was very sick. But they did manage to take their first two Prussian prisoners, before they moved to a support position. They then moved into line, where they faced shells and a 'Boche strafe', but they also received "strawberries, cherries and cream from Paris!!!" sent by the 25th division. They were relieved by an Italian Garibaldi regiment "with their red handkerchiefs projecting from their left breast pockets", whose commander had been Secretary of the State Railways in Rome.

Geoffrey's sciatica had begun to cause him problems again, but an expected German attack in mid-July failed to materialize, due probably to a torrential downpour, and he was able to go on leave for two weeks and rejoin the family. While in England he saw Louis, who had become vicar of Hennock in Devon, together with his wife, Olive, and their daughters Elizabeth, born in 1916, and Marian, born

119

the following year. He also dined with Roger in Taunton.

There were now only two months of the war left and Geoffrey had completed a year in France. Having relieved the Royal Scots in the front line in the Koudekot sector, they witnessed great activity in the air, and the Germans counter-attacked the division on their left. One day "three prisoners walked into my lines in the early morning – Alsatians aged 19, two of whom spoke French well." The lines were then relieved but, while they were resting, the battalion mounted an attack taking 50 prisoners, and then faced much heavy gunning and a German counter-attack, which resulted in about 130 casualties.

By the end of August the "Boche were retiring on our front as expected" and "we made a good advance" over the next few days. Geoffrey had a "narrow escape from a 4.2 shell which killed Sergeant Mallin, wounded Beale (my adjutant) and two others (out of a group of five). I alone was untouched." The battalion moved forward in support of the 7/8th Inniskillings before withdrawing to the slopes of Kemmel, where they faced heavy shelling all night. They then went back to brigade support, but Geoffrey writes in his war diary that "I was relieved of command". "This was caused by my talking too straight to the Acting Brigadier (Colonel Irvine 7/8 Inniskillings) going back to report the situation in the front line, that of the 7/8 Inniskillings being positively dangerous!!"

The final weeks of the war were spent with the 2nd Army Musketry School, where new recruits were put through their paces with parades and work on the ranges. On 8 November he joined in a 'peace' drink at HQ mess "as the civilians think peace has been signed and are hanging flags out". Three days later on 11 November he wrote that "Germans have signed terms of armistice and firing is to cease at 11 a.m. today!!!! All the villages in the district are ringing their bells and there is general rejoicing!!" The next day there was a "parade of children with flags and 'Jack' (a dog) decorated with French colours".

CHAPTER TWELVE

NEW MOVES IN THE INTER-WAR YEARS

Roger was demobilised in February 1919 and the family moved from Pleasley back to Limehurst for a short time. There he and Helen made a key decision that they did not want to spend the rest of their lives at Wall near Lichfield and therefore sold the house.

This was because "the call of the West Country was strong, and remembering the attractions of Somerset, we looked out for a house in that county. An advertisement for Creech Barrow House took us to Taunton, but the agent assured us that the house would not suit us, and suggested our looking at one at Crowcombe Heathfield." This was a house that had been built just before the war, but had never been inhabited. "It seemed cheap and about the right size for us, so we bought it and moved in on March 14. There was some heath land, adjoining the station, which went with the house, and I bought a few Exmoor ponies at Lord Poltimore's sale, and ran them there. A little later we built on a couple of octagonal-shaped rooms to the house, which we called 'Wall House'. For transport I got hold of a four-wheeled dog-cart, and later a second-hand Hupmobile car" while the children had an Exmoor pony. On Sundays the children walked to church through the muddy Somerset lanes and when they returned their boots were filthy, but fortunately they had servants to clean their boots and to ensure that the Sunday lunch was being cooked.

Roger became a JP in 1923, a position that he continued to hold when they moved again the following year. This occurred because "we had an opportunity of buying 'Higher House', Bagborough, with about 50 acres of land, so we sold Crowcombe House and took the name of 'Wall House' with us. I designed a large addition to the new house, and we moved there on October 13. Because of a builders' strike, the house was not finished by the day we had to move in, and we spent an uncomfortable few days until the men moved out. There were glorious views from the house; on one clear day I identified no

121

less than 27 churches from a point in the garden." The ponies were now kept on the Quantocks in the summer and driven down again before the winter. This was great fun for the children who helped by opening gates and ensuring that they were driven the right way.

Geoffrey returned from France at the end of March 1919 and by then Olive was anxious to move from their house in Ashburton. They looked at some other houses, one particularly charming, but unfortunately the owner, the county surveyor, would not sell. They could not find anything suitable until June 1920 when they moved into Moor House on the outskirts of Totnes.

However, in April 1921 their peace was disturbed when orders were received to mobilize in order to deal with strikes and Geoffrey, being on the reserve of officers, had to report to Warrington for strike duty. He remained at the depot in charge of the reservists, many of whom came from the London district and had well-paid jobs. "They found the small amount of army pay totally inadequate for their families, and there was a great state of unrest. I had an exceptionally trying time, receiving countless letters from the men's wives appealing for the return of their men. At last the War Office decided that a percentage of extra hard cases should be released, and I had to spend endless hours going through the letters and deciding which were the hardest cases. This, I think, was undoubtedly the most unpleasant period in my soldiering career, but relief came in a most unexpected way. Playing tennis, I was making a backhand stroke on the base line, when I ruptured a calf muscle." It turned out to be a "blessing in disguise, for I was naturally relieved of further duty".

After a spell in the Millbank Military Hospital in London, he was able to return to Totnes where he and Olive remained until October 1924, when they left Moor House and went into rooms, before renting a bungalow at Lustleigh for three months at the end of the year. This was because they had bought their own bungalow under Lustleigh Cleave which needed alterations and, on the last day of the year, they went to inspect progress on the foundations for the new rooms that they were having built, including a larger bathroom and stairs leading to two new rooms in the roof. Some granite rock had had to be blasted in the hillside to help the excavations. The work was completed by April 1925 when they moved in to their new bungalow which they called 'Rock-Holt', afterwards known as

CHAPTER THIRTEEN

HUNTING

For both Roger and Geoffrey hunting played an integral part in their lives. But for them, it was not the traditional image of hunting on horseback, it was hunting on foot, for otter in summer and fox or hare in the winter. Geoffrey wrote that "with slender resources most of my hunting has been on foot, but this has been by no means a handicap, as with a stout pair of legs and a good wind I have been able to last through the day 'till I was 68!" Both he and Roger threw all their energy into hunting, travelling vast distances, and taking every opportunity to go hunting all over the country. Geoffrey wrote that "with a certain amount of the hunting instinct, and if one uses one's head, it is amazing what a lot of houndwork one can enjoy. With the aid of a one inch Ordnance Survey map it is possible to keep with hounds throughout the day, even in a completely strange country."

Two examples of the amazing distances which they covered on foot in a day occurred just a fortnight apart in 1923, when Roger was 46 and Geoffrey was 45. On 15 December Geoffrey took the early train to Moretonhampstead, cycled out eight miles to the Warren Inn, and then ran on over the moor for several miles to the meet of the South Devon Foxhounds at Tawton Gate. During the day a fox, ran a ten-mile point from Stonetor Hill to Buckland Beacon, 13 or 14 miles as hounds ran, in 1 hour 34 minutes, before escaping in a clitter of rocks.[55] Geoffrey got there only six minutes after the hounds, having covered the distance on foot, a remarkable achievement when one considers the terrain that he was covering over the middle of Dartmoor. He then jogged back to the meet with hounds afterwards. On 27 December Roger wrote to Geoffrey "I followed your great hunt of the week before last with great interest on the ordnance map. It was a noteworthy performance. However I'm not at all sure that I can't cap it! Yesterday I had the greatest run I've had, certainly for 12

---

[55] Impenetrable rocks found on Dartmoor.

131

years, and for pace and length combined probably the best I ever took part in!" He had been out hunting two days earlier and wasn't sure how well he would get through, but "I proved to be wonderfully fit". To get to the meet "I walked seven miles and got a lift for the last eight". Hounds had a hunt of 1 hour 50 minutes before they caught their fox, a point of nine miles and between 15 and 20 as hounds ran. "I had the hardest possible work to keep anywhere near them, but I ran faster – far faster – than I care for, and measuring my route I find that I went 15 miles in 2 hours five minutes! So I'm fitter than I suspected." Having done all this "I jogged seven miles to Wiveliscombe" before he was given a lift home.

But this sort of thing was not exceptional for them. In June 1924, in order to go hunting in Cornwall, Geoffrey rose at 3.45 a.m., left Totnes on bicycle at 5.15, caught a train at 7.45 and left it at Saltash, cycling on to Linkinhorne. This amounted to 38 miles actual riding on bicycle, after which he ran on three miles to the meet. He then walked all day with the hounds.

In March 1926 Roger wrote to Geoffrey that, when staying near Oxford, he took his stepmother's brother Richard Hill and their daughter Doreen out to a meet of the Avon Vale Foxhounds. During the day they "had a very nice run of an hour and nine minutes, during which the fox crossed the River Avon, near Chippenham. Only 8 riders crossed the river, the rest going many miles round to a bridge. I went across (the river on foot) holding a good fellow's hand – otherwise I would have been washed away! On the far side (of the river) I had most of it to myself, owing to barbed wire in *every* fence (which impeded the riders) and the hounds eventually marked the fox to ground. Not bad for an old un! Then I ran six miles in the hour back to the car where I had appointed a *rendezvous* with the others at three. So home, bathed and tea'd and on here (Wall House, Bagborough) for dinner. *Very* tired today, but slept an hour after lunch."

Roger explained the art of hunting on foot in his pantomime when a character called Willie Till – a hunt runner – says:

You've got to be in training if you want to run to hounds
You must learn to know the meaning of the various hunting sounds.
You must pay attention to the circling of the birds,
And the agitated movements of the excited flocks and herds.

Remember it's the pace that kills, and don't push on too quick,
You must watch how hounds are turning, and be ready for a nick
Be determined to be with them, and I'll guarantee you'll find
When the longest run is over that you won't be far behind.

Roger had first hunted hounds when he formed the South
Bedfordshire Foot Beagles to hunt hares when he was living at
Ampthill Grange in 1904. When the pack was started Roger wrote
that "as the continuance of the pack is mainly dependent upon the
goodwill of the farmers, it is earnestly requested that those who
come out will see that gates are not left open and that no unneces-
sary gaps (in hedges) are made." He also hoped that the "following
points will be observed by all who come out:- do not holloa when a
hare is seen, but hold up a hat or handkerchief" and "when hounds
check, stand still and avoid talking loudly."

Roger says that he "had a tremendous lot of fun with them". On
one occasion, when they met near Woburn Abbey, Geoffrey records
that "hares were altogether too plentiful and we kept running into
the Duke of Bedford's coverts which were full of brambles and
fresh hares." But in November 1905 when he spent much of his
leave at Ampthill and went hunting with Roger's beagles, the best
day was from Hockliffe Grange when they had a run at great pace
and an excellent hunt before catching their hare.

But for both of them their first love was otter hunting. A famous
West Country professional huntsman, Phil Back, said to Geoffrey "I
reckon I know pretty well all there is to be known about a fox, but
there's a lot I have to learn about an otter." Both Roger and Geoffrey
knew an awful lot about otters, but neither would boast an intimate
knowledge. Geoffrey's view was as true then as it still is today that
"no British mammal is less understood than *lutra vulgaris*".

But for Roger and Geoffrey "a great part of the fascination of
otter-hunting" was "that one is constantly learning, and yet trying to
learn still more". They both went otter hunting before reaching their
teens, they both saw a large number of packs, and they both studied
closely the methods employed by the best huntsmen of their day.
Geoffrey feels that they owed most to Captain Sheppard, who hunted
the King's Otter Hounds in Ireland. His hunting diaries "were unri-
valled" and "my brother and myself were influenced almost as much
by the constant reading of them, as we were by his most instructive

133

and enjoyable companionship. Indeed our thoughts and ideas on the sport became so welded, as it were, and so similar, that when we came to carry the horn with the old pack we had been brought up with (the Dartmoor Otter Hounds), we were able to provide sport of a high standard."

The Devon and Cornwall rivers hunted by the Dartmoor Otter Hounds presented a special challenge to a huntsman because of the fast-flowing rocky rivers, lots of rocky clitters, and the lack of scent for hounds, especially when conditions were cold and wet.

Roger and Geoffrey were both well-suited to meet this challenge. They had a very good appreciation of hounds and houndwork, of the habits of otters and a knowledge of the rivers and countryside, which was so necessary if they were not to pass over otters which was all too easy to do. Geoffrey maintained that the best huntsman is the one who "passes over the fewest otters".

In all this they were both fortunate to inherit a good pack of hounds, for breeding is not something that can be developed overnight, but they also used their own skills and powers of observation. On so many occasions in their diaries they show how they were able to observe one hound which showed an interest in a place where the otter was, when it had been passed over by the rest of the pack.

They were, like all huntsmen, concerned to catch their quarry, but they disapproved of what they considered to be the less sporting practices of their day and were concerned to give the otter every chance by giving them 'law' – a few minutes to get a head start.

The first time that Geoffrey hunted a pack of hounds was in Ireland in 1911 when he was asked to do so by the master David Kent. Having found and caught an otter "a highly excited Irish lad then ran up to me to say that there was another otter back in the pool. To be quite honest, I hardly credited him, knowing how readily the Irish will holloa a large salmon for an otter. However, this proved quite genuine" and hounds hunted him for three hours until David Kent said "spare him yer honour" which they did.

Roger became Master of the Northern Counties Otter Hounds in 1913 and hunted them throughout what proved to be a most successful season. Geoffrey and Louis stayed in Northumberland for a few days in August when they found otters at Bolham Lake, west of Morpeth and on the Coquet at Guyzance near Warkworth and at Chatheugh Island upstream from Acklington Bridge.

The inter-war years saw both brothers hunt the Dartmoor Otter

Hounds. Geoffrey was the first to hunt the pack in July 1926 in unusual circumstances. On finishing hunting he 'bade farewell' to Jack Goodwin, the current master on 3 July "little thinking that I should never see him again alive, for he appeared hale and hearty and tough as ever". Two days later he heard that he was dead. He had apparently been stung in the throat by a poisonous fly and had refused to have a doctor. "He apparently choked last night and was found dead against his bed." Geoffrey wrote that he was "terribly depressed and sad at the loss of one of my best friends and a rare sportsman".

Geoffrey was invited to hunt hounds, but wrote that "I could not afford to do the whole season" so it was arranged that he should share it with his old friend Jim Wolferstan. The first day that he hunted hounds on the River Tavy, Roger was out as well and they found an otter which they left after a long hunt. A few days later with Roger and his eldest son Charles, and Olive present at the meet at Bodmin Road Station, they had a long downstream hunt in the course of which Geoffrey lost the horn that he had used in the charge at Gallipoli in rapid water. Fortunately it was retrieved later.

It was agreed that the arrangement should continue for the following season with Geoffrey's out-of-pocket expenses being paid out of hunt funds. In June hounds found an otter near Lanhydrock in Cornwall and had a great hunt, until the acting master said they had to call off to catch a train. A few days later otters were found in Staverton weir pool and Kilbury weir pool near Buckfastleigh, both on the River Dart. At the end of the season in early October they had a good hunt on the River Avon near Gara Bridge, despite the river being high and very cold.

1928 was the final year of this arrangement, where the hunting was shared, and in June Geoffrey had a very pleasing hunt on the River Fowey, after meeting at Lostwithiel, but two days later he was seized with an attack of appendicitis and had to take things easy for a while. During the course of a hunt on the Camel he saw an otter make a six-foot dive into a weir pool.

Geoffrey hunted hounds on his own in 1929, as Jim Wolferstan was suffering from ill-health. In June he writes that "I was particularly anxious to show the field a good day on the River Bovey and if possible to have a hunt on the lovely Parke stretch belonging to my cousin Major Willie Hole. As we reached the pond at Parke hounds gave tongue on the old crossing place to the river." This led to a mark 200 yards above the weir pool and "the cry in these lovely woodlands was superb as hounds swam their otter upwards." They found no less than four otters on the river that day.

The Western Morning News report of the season said that it "will go down in history as one of the best in its existence". Geoffrey wrote that "I feel that I was indeed fortunate to have hunted such a pack for three-and-a-half seasons", but that "I was sad at having to hang up my horn all too soon owing to financial circumstances. These I explained to the committee at a meeting when I regretfully tended my resignation as honorary huntsman and was thanked for my services."

But he was pleased that Roger did have the finances to become Master of the Dartmoor Otter Hounds, a position which he held for the next three years. Roger wrote "what a happy three seasons they were". He was then living at Bagborough in Somerset but set off "quite early – often with one of the boys to whip in – and it was grand driving along the empty roads to the various meets. Sometimes it meant staying out for a few nights." Travel during this 1930 season was made easier "by the acquisition of a motor hound-van" for the first time.

This first year was noted for a succession of floods which started at the beginning of August and affected the rest of the season. "One of the most thrilling drags was that enjoyed on the Fowey from Lostwithiel when the pack covered themselves with glory by battling against a raging flood for an hour or more, till they came up with a brace of otters and killed one of them." The Western Morning News reported that "among the outstanding hunts of the season, that which was enacted on Kitley Pond easily heads the list. For seven hours 40 minutes the pack were engaged with a brace of otters on this beautiful sheet of water. It was undoubtedly the best scent of the season, and all those who were fortunate to be present are agreed that never before had they listened to so rich and continuous a chorus as that to which they were treated on that occasion."

Perhaps the most thrilling hunt of the 1931 season was on the West Looe river in Cornwall. The otter was given five minutes 'law' before hounds were laid on and went down the water "on a rare scent, crashed through Canakey Wood, and returned to water below the pond. There was short spell of difficult hunting, up and down a muddy leat, terminating in the otter getting behind the mill wheel."

Then he landed again, crossed the river and turned up the steep hill through Trenchway Hill, near the top of which he was killed before he could reach some big badger earths.

Roger's final year 1932 was "a remarkable one" with more otters being found – 60- than any other season since the pack had been formed. The most remarkable hunt was that on the River Tavy from Lopwell when they found one under Buckland Abbey "rattled him up and down the water and then he took a very long excursion through the woods almost to Denham Bridge. After that he refused to stay long in the river and landed over and over again, to run the thick brambles on the right bank. Next he went down to Coffee Pot pool, but soon tired of the water, came back overland through the woods on the right bank." "He must have been an exceptionally strong and fit otter; he was just as much on land as in the water and the music was loud and continuous throughout. The end came on a shallow just below the bramble-patch."

The report of the season in Horse and Hound ended "report has it that Major R.J.K. Mott has definitely decided to lay up his horn, and his place will be hard indeed to fill in this most sporting of all countries."

Both brothers had always sought opportunities to go hunting. When sending letters home at the time of the Boer War, Roger wrote "would that I were off to 'The Three Pigeons' tomorrow" (a famous meet of the South Oxfordshire Foxhounds); or that "I don't think I shall be home by June; it will more probably be October – in time for the hunting season!" While Geoffrey, when asked whether he "managed to work in a hunt in France" during the First World War, said "the answer is unfortunately 'no', for although we had a number of hunting men serving, it was just not possible." But even if it was not possible in these conditions, it *was* practically everywhere else he went!

They also liked to spread their views to others and Geoffrey was hunting correspondent to many publications, The Times, Horse and Hound and the Western Times ending his reports with his *nom de plume* 'Clinker' taken from the name of his best hound with the Dartmoor Otter Hounds.

But although hunting played such a big part in their lives, and although they firmly believed that the best way to preserve otters and foxes and otters was to hunt them so that landowners and water bailiffs would encourage their habitats and not shoot or trap them, they were also good countrymen who got on with others, even if they did not share their views on hunting. Geoffrey tells of one such man called Graham who had a lovely house on a small brook – a tributary of the River Hems, often used by otters. He was "a shy type of man and objected to hounds invading his property. When Jack Goodwin was master I suggested that I should go and interview Graham and see if I could not persuade him to let us hunt his water. Goodwin told me that I might as well talk to a brick wall. However, I went, and leaving my cycle half way up his drive, walked on to the house and rang the bell. His housekeeper came out and, telling me he was in the garden, clanged a large bell and went in search of him."

"Returning, she showed me into a somewhat bare room with old college groups hanging on the walls. After a while she came in and ushered me into the study where I introduced myself and explained the reason for my visit. He at once told me he did not want hounds, as he quite disliked taking life in any shape or form. I replied that I quite understood, and added "I see you were at the House" (his college being Christ Church, Oxford) and "we talked about Oxford. Then I noticed a spray of some rather rare shrub on his mantelpiece, mentioning its name. He asked me if I was interested in gardens and I told him it was my next keenest hobby to hunting. The sequel was a drink or two and a stroll round the garden, after which, on my declining an invitation to lunch, he suggested walking with me to where I had left my bicycle. Pointing to his stream I asked him if there were any big trout in it. His eyes sparkled as he said "Yes indeed one of my greatest pleasures is feeding them." When I asked what he fed them on he replied "wasp grubs". Quickly grasping my opportunity I said in a horrified tone "you do not mean to say that you take the life of a poor little wasp?" "Oh" he replied "you can bring your hounds here, but give me 24 hours notice, so that I shall not be present!"

"Not only did I most carefully carry out his wishes whenever we met in his neighbourhood but I also looked him up from time to time, and so this aesthetic old bachelor and I became good friends" with the result that when he died he left Geoffrey a full-plate stand camera in his will.

CHAPTER FOURTEEN

THE SECOND WORLD WAR AND THE 1950s

By the beginning of 1939 Roger "hankered for the West Country" so he and Helen sold Allum Green which was occupied by troops. "The house was hit by a bomb" in 1940 because the troops had not dealt with the 'black-out' efficiently and four soldiers were killed. Roger and Helen moved to the Bell House in Trull, near Taunton in March 1939.

In April 1940 Roger joined the 'Local Defence Volunteers' – later called the Home Guard – as a platoon commander of the Blagdon Hill Company, "my areas being the parishes of Trull, Pitminster, and Angersleigh". "Something like 300 men" joined the platoon during the course of the war and Roger used to form them up outside the Winchester Arms and drill them in the car park. There is a photograph of the company taken in a field by Fullwood Farm in which 67 men are parading at attention in uniform with their rifles, apart from their two commanding officers, including Roger, who did not carry rifles.

When invasion was felt to be imminent in September 1940, at the time of the Battle of Britain, the general staff issued a prearranged code-word to all Home Guard units – 'Cromwell'. There was a false alarm that night and the church bells of Trull and Pitminster were rung in expectation of invasion and road blocks and vulnerable points were manned by villagers, ready to fight. But the next day they were dismissed and the order was given to 'be at the ready'. The Somerset County Gazette reported that "the mistaken alarm of an attempt at invasion in the west of England aroused last weekend by the ringing of church bells in many villages and towns had one good effect that has given satisfaction to those responsible for our defence forces. This was the smartness with which the Home Guard responded to the emergency with which every post was manned in the shortest possible time." Whether the reality really matched up to this is open to doubt, as at least one member of Roger's platoon had

139

to rush out to his post in such a hurry that he did not have time to put his boots on!

A code-word played its part on another occasion, when, out on exercise, Roger tripped over one of his men in the dark who called out his name 'Churchill'. As this was the current code-word and thinking that there was an emergency, the alarm was sounded and everyone was called out!

Geoffrey applied to the War Office for a combatant job when the war started but they would not give him one because of his age – 63. However, in May 1940 he was asked to form a platoon of Local Defence Volunteers which he did. Two months later the platoon was made part of a company, with Geoffrey now in overall command of six platoons. As a result he had to organize the platoons, issue rifles, ammunition and stores, and arrange observation posts and road blocks. This meant plenty of office work during the day and platoons to be inspected in the evenings. There were also plenty of battalion conferences to attend and arrangements to be made for lectures and training.

But the war came much closer to home in January 1941 when "I made an amazing discovery in my garden. Finding a wire resting on my telephone wire in the orchard and several coils of wire round my main gate, I rang up the Royal Engineers and police. The police came shortly after to report a small parachute at the north end of the wire on Mapstone Hill. I then made a search in the other direction and found in the wood some 50 yards above our house a small yellow cylindrical bomb dangling from a tree 15 ft above the ground! Two officers of the Bomb Disposal Unit came and took the bomb down and exploded it."

Otherwise training continued with machine gun posts being constructed, inspections of service respirators and search light posts and a road block demonstration. When there was a section competition his No 1 and No 2 platoons won the bombing, drill and shooting elements. There were also some larger scale exercises, such as one at Chagford which went off very well. Their training was put into practice when a German plane crashed near Dunsford and "two prisoners were captured by my No 1 Platoon, two of the crew were killed. These were the first prisoners to be taken by the battalion." Lustleigh also suffered its first bombing, but the inhabitants gave an entertainment and supper to the Home Guard at the beginning of 1942 "which was greatly appreciated".

All this Home Guard work kept Geoffrey very busy but, by the autumn of 1942, "having been considerably troubled with my eyesight and so much office work, I decided to resign from the Home Guard after two-and-a-half years." He now took over the post of people's warden at Lustleigh. Louis, meanwhile, combined his clerical duties as vicar of Chudleigh Knighton with those of a special constable and Geoffrey took snapshots of him "doing point duty near the market in Newton Abbot".

At the end of 1943 Geoffrey was "the principal guest at a Home Guard supper" and he attended the final 'stand-down' parade at Bovey Tracey in December 1944. Having stepped down from the Home Guard, he had more time for his garden and for discussions with the botanist Keble Martin who "mentioned two plants growing in our district – *lobelia urens* and *dianthus armeria*". Geoffrey sent him specimens of *ophioglossum* (adder's tongue) and *erodium cicutarium*. He also planted *acers* in his garden to commemorate his sons getting their commissions and a *cotoneaster salicifolia* to commemorate their wedding anniversary. 3 August 1944 was the 46th anniversary of their first meeting at Bow Bridge, Harbertonford at a 4 a.m meeting of the Dartmoor Otter Hounds.

Roger and Helen had two sons who played particular roles in the war. Antony, like his father and grandfather, served in the Queen's Royal Regiment, in his case the first regiment.[56] He was promoted to the rank of captain and then major in 1941 and returned to England in 1943 after being mentioned in despatches for his part in operations in command of D company at Razmak on the North West frontier.

He took part in the D-Day landings on 6 June 1944, where having "landed in water about seven feet deep", he managed to catch hold of a chain on a landing craft and got towed ashore. Some men were hit by mortars, but he managed to get the rest of the men off the beach, using the cover provided by five-foot high reeds. One by one his men and fellow officers were killed but he stuck to his task to push on to Asnelles. When a fellow officer, Graham Elliott, dashed into a crater "as no one went with him I did" and when a stick

---

[56] In 1921 The Queen's (Royal West Surrey) Regiment was restyled The Queen's Royal Regiment (West Surrey).

grenade exploded, "Graham bravely hurled his body on top of me". It was a dangerous time. "At one time I saw two Boche through a gap, so fired shots at them, and the next day found two corpses with bullets through their heads – only 20 yards range." After that "I took my men into Asnelles without seeing anyone". But "suddenly I felt a blast and heard a loud crack and splinters came off the road into my face … then came another blast and another and it dawned on me that there was an anti-tank gun in our way." Graham was killed and it took an armoured vehicle to silence the opposition. His next job was more pleasant, taking his company into Arromanches where the people were "delighted to see us and where "the only opposition was from a dog, presumably a Boche one!"

During the subsequent days he was at times "fairly well in the thick of things" and casualties remained high. On 19 June, as it was starting to get dark, he "started to go through a gap in the hedge, when a flash, a sharp crack and I was bowled over into the road." He was dressed and put in an ambulance, told someone had put "evacuate" on my label" and was flown out in a Dakota eventually ending up in Derbyshire Royal Infirmary.

Roger's youngest son, David, was appointed as lieutenant on the submarine *Rorqual* in 1939 off Singapore, before moving to operations in the Mediterranean in 1940-1. He was awarded the Distinguished Service Cross "for courage and skill during successful submarine operations". When he left the ship his commander said that "I have every confidence that he will … go far in the service". He then went to the submarine *Taku* and a few months later came home on leave and married Sheila Prentice, whom he had met while living at Allum Green. He returned to service in the Mediterranean and, on leaving *Taku*, was described as "an able young officer" who "should make a successful submarine commanding officer, for which he is highly recommended". He commanded the submarines *Otway* and *H 44*, before taking over *Usurper*, which was lost in November 1943. Rear-Admiral Barry wrote to Sheila "I wish I could give you some news regarding the loss, but we just know nothing about it, except that the submarine has gone."

The other children were nearer to home. Sylvia and her children came to live at the Bell House for some of the time when her daughter Rosemary was born, but for most of the war she lived at a house in Kingston St Mary near Taunton, while her husband Humphry was on active service with his regiment in Northern India. He fought in the Burma Campaign, including the Battle of Kohima in 1944.Charles went onto the Reserve List of Officers after August 1939 when he joined the supply depot in Taunton. In December 1944 he was married to Elsa in Trull church.

Meanwhile Geoffrey's son John, who was in India, could not join up until the tea company he worked for released him. But in 1942 he was transferred to the Gurkhas and, having done jungle training, "went through the Burma campaign with them". He was in action for the first time at Thazi. His other son, Raymond, was based at Kohima and Mandalay. Both sons were promoted to the rank of captain.

Hunting could not continue during the war and the last three of the Dartmoor Otter Hounds had to be put down in December 1944. It therefore had to be revived after the war and Roger took over as master of the neighbouring Culmstock Otter Hounds which he hunted with a small pack of hounds. The Dartmoor Otter Hounds did not resume regular hunting until 1952 and they had to rely on visits from neighbouring packs, including the Culmstock. So when in 1948 the Royal Naval College, Dartmouth rang Geoffrey "asking if I could arrange an otter hunt for the cadets I readily agreed" the result was a special meet of the Culmstock. Roger's pack found two otters and "the cadets thoroughly enjoyed their day".

Two months later Geoffrey, suffering from colitis, was taken to hospital in Exeter where 'Operation Otter' was performed. While waiting to be dressed for the operation, he wrote a hunting article for the Daily Telegraph. "Next morning the surgeon told me that everything had gone off extremely well." He was later told that two thirds of his colon and six inches of the ileum had been removed. He had lost three-and-a-half stones but was discharged a week earlier than expected. Two months later he had put on two stones.

Geoffrey writes that "everything had gone well during 1949 until December 20, when just as we had finished tea my poor Olive had most severe pains in the head, and our new doctor lost no time in coming to her assistance, and took endless trouble to ease her sufferings. I sat up with her all night and Louis brought Mary Weston over next morning who was most helpful until the ambulance arrived and we took her to the Cottage Hospital at Moretonhamstead. The following evening I was told that she was speaking more clearly."

By January there was "a very great improvement in Olive's condition" and she was taken from hospital to Bovey Tracey to convalesce. But "a few days after her arrival there she had a rather serious setback, but happily the district nurse was on the spot" and the doctor "gave her quick relief". It was not until March that she was able to come home after an absence of over ten weeks.

By April her "health was beginning to improve, and she was able to enjoy short walks" and by August she was able to walk to the village and back. The following year in June they stayed at Sidmouth where "the change seemed to do Olive good" but at the end of July "she developed glaucoma in her right eye" and was taken by ambulance to Exeter Eye Infirmary, where it was decided that a draining operation was necessary. She did not return home until September.

Geoffrey and Olive celebrated their 47th wedding anniversary in January 1952 with lunch at a hotel, when Olive seemed better, but a few days later "she took a turn for the worse, and the doctor brought a nurse early the following morning who told me that her condition was critical." Six days later Sister Armour "took me into see Olive and told me that she was sinking fast … and she passed away peacefully in her sleep."

After a short and bright service in Lustleigh Church, Louis read the committal at the crematorium in Plymouth. Geoffrey made up a family wreath with flowers from their garden "the loveliest I could find".

Meanwhile at the end of August 1951 Roger's days as Master of the Culmstock Otter Hounds came to a sudden end, when he had a coronary thrombosis and was taken by ambulance to a nursing home. Geoffrey said that "it was a very severe attack and I was unable to see him until September when, happily, I found he was making a splendid recovery and was very cheery and in good heart." He was able to return home after seven weeks in the nursing home.

When Geoffrey visited him and Helen at the Bell House in March 1954 to celebrate his 77th birthday, "he was looking very fit." Geoffrey stayed with them again in October 1954 and the two brothers were together again the following year for Roger's birthday. Roger, who had been churchwarden of Trull since 1943, was now able to implement a scheme to rid the church of death-watch beetle, to have it cleaned and repainted and for the lighting to be renewed. He was also very much involved in plans for a new memorial hall saying at the beginning of July 1956 that we do not want a makeshift structure, but must "build a hall of which we shall be proud".

In May 1956 all three brothers were together at the opening meet of the Dartmoor Otter Hounds at Parke, Bovey Tracey and, when the same pack met in July, both Roger and Geoffrey were out and Roger got the first view of a big otter. Geoffrey stayed in one spot watching for the otter and "Roger came down to me .... once or twice, and we discussed the hunt. He apparently left about 4 p.m. and caught the 4.25 p.m. train at Loddeswell for Gara Bridge (where he had left his car in the morning). The porter said he was apparently quite well and active as he boarded the train, but he was found dead in his carriage by the guard when the train arrived at Gara Bridge (only an eight-minute journey). He had refused my offer (and that of two others) of a lift to the train or back to his car." Geoffrey says that "he may have taken the hill up to the station too fast" but that "looking back one cannot help thinking what a wonderful finish it was to a sporting life, although, of course, a great shock for Helen and the family. He and I were always the best of friends, frequently hunted together, and kept up a regular correspondence, and life has never been the same for me since his passing." A memorial service was held for him in Trull church, taken by the vicar Charles Trevelyan, who had taught at Wellington College and was a great friend of the family. The church was full of relations, sporting friends and representatives of local bodies.

Two other deaths which occurred in these years were those of Edward and Walter Parlby, the last surviving brothers of Gertrude - Roger, Geoffrey and Louis' mother. Edward died in October 1951, while Walter died in Canada in January 1952. A few years earlier Geoffrey and Olive had been to Scotland to stay with their Parlby cousins Jack and Dot Arbuthnott, but Geoffrey had little success with fishing, the weather was against them and the river was over its banks. The country was also too waterlogged for the Highland Games to take place, which was unfortunate as they had got seats in the royal enclosure.

After Olive's death Geoffrey decided to sell the house at Lustleigh "the best home we ever had during our married life" after 29 years and move into rooms. When clearing out his things he "came across some old uniform and decided to present it to the Royal Theatre, Exeter". But when he was waiting to see the manager "I noticed on either side of his office entrance door two theatrical 'bills'. One of these dated back to 1872, and gave particulars of a play (*A Hun-*

145

dred Thousand Pounds) in which my father took the lead! (as General Goodwin). I asked the manager why it had been preserved all these years, and he pointed out that it had been a charity performance and that the Lord Mayor of London was patron."

Geoffrey also travelled more and returned to Ireland on a number of occasions. When he went with his son Raymond to a meet of the Cork City Otter Hounds, he was told that "a bus would leave the Opera House at noon. So thither we went and found men arriving with single hounds on leashes and Eddy White the honorary secretary who was to hunt hounds in the master's absence. There was no uniform and Eddy was dressed in a chocolate coloured trouser suit! He gave us a cheery welcome and asked us to join them on the bus. He took a 'cap' on the bus, but when I offered him a contribution he refused to take anything saying "shure, you're our guests". When I wished him good luck he told me rather gloomily that he was afraid otters were rather scarce. However, hounds were keen enough when put to water, and some 500 yards above the bridge they put off an otter lying rough, and a monster he was! I was fortunate enough to get the first view. Hounds pressed from the start and he soon landed across a road and entered a gorse covert. The chorus from the hounds was terrific here and he presently returned to the river and after two hours hounds lost touch with him. Eddy came up to me and said "he has us beat".

On a subsequent visit the Welfort Beagles met on the banks of Lough Rea and Geoffrey met the lady master, "her smart little pack and two ladies whipping-in. There were several hares afoot, but scent on so warm a day was all too catchy. We thoroughly enjoyed watching the young lasses leaping over the dykes and we filled them up with cider at the end of the day."

Ireland featured again in 1958 when arrangements were made for Geoffrey to have a day's hunting on his 80th birthday, which fell on a Sunday and therefore he could not hunt in England. The 'Peterborough' columnist of the Daily Telegraph contacted him about his plans for his birthday and these appeared the next day in the 'London Day by Day' section.

On the day itself his Irish hosts "drank my health, and then I cut an enormous cake, with 80 candles on a board beside it. We then went into the yard where, at noon, Paddy Manning, the master (incidentally the local road man) arrived with his keen little pack. He

146

introduced me to his pals, and more toasts were drunk before moving off. We were not more than 200 yards from the entrance gate when, before they left the lane, the pack were in full cry. 'They've found' said Joan (his hostess) and indeed they had, but never a fox or hare was it, but a great roaming sheepdog who was lucky to get away as he gained the shelter of his own farm yard after a sharp ten minutes!"

"Paddy then took the pack into a rough dingle with steep slopes and on the one side very thick covert where they came on a fox, but soon changed on to a hare, and ran for some distance over open country before they could be stopped. Returning to the dingle a full chorus announced another find. This time it was a good stout fox who took them up and down the valley several times, until he was finally forced to leave and make for the cliffs. It was quite a memorable day and a highly amusing one."

Four days later he went to hunt with the Carbery Hounds. "The brothers O'Driscoll were then masters. The elder brother carried the horn and was rather dour, but the younger was exceedingly cheery. To my amazement he said to me 'Sure I have a lot of mail for ye'!! And indeed he had, for next day I received a packet of 30 birthday cards which he forwarded on to me."

At the end of his trip he was visiting a friend, Ikey Bell, who was suffering from influenza when "the front door bell rang and the nurse ushered in four brawny Irishmen, who turned out to be members of the Bride View Otter Hunt. Ikey and I were sitting in armchairs, and these four stood in front of us and said the hotel folk had told them I was there, and they wanted me to go back to the hotel and talk of 'The Old Days'! Ikey persuaded me to go, saying they would take it badly if I did not. So to the hotel we went, and for a full two hours they kept me talking, mostly of the day I hunted their hounds on the River Bride at Castle Lyons in September 1911 and of the wonderful hunt we had." This was the occasion 47 years ago when he first hunted a pack of hounds.

CHAPTER FIFTEEN

POSTSCRIPT

Geoffrey lived to see his 100th birthday and became a celebrated character in the circles in which he moved. In 1963 he was invited to the ceremony of presenting new colours to his battalion at Warrington by the Lord Lieutenant, Lord Derby. He had been adjutant in 1909 when King Edward VII presented the last colours and writes that he found himself treated as a VIP and "was given the seat next to the saluting base".

When he was 88, he and his brother Louis went to a Buckingham Palace garden party, where they were joined by other Boer War veterans. Geoffrey remembers that the veterans were "given special prominence, and the Queen gave us her sweetest smile as she shook hands with each one of us. I was the senior officer present and Her Majesty asked what regiment I was with in South Africa and I replied "The Fighting Fortieth ma'am". Three days later he paraded at Chelsea Barracks, where the veterans were inspected by the Queen Mother. "She was very charming and apologized for being late. I managed to get our detachment on the right of the front line, and when she came up to me she said 'I hope you have not been standing too long', and I replied 'I would stand forever for you ma'am'. And this drew a second lovely smile from her."

When he was 92, "owing to so much lawlessness in the country, the police insisted on depriving me of my old revolver, which I have carried in every campaign I have been in." By the time of his 94th birthday there were only 100 of the Boer War veterans still alive.

On his 95th birthday, the BBC turned up to mark the occasion by interviewing him at the meet of the Heythrop Hunt with "countless photographs being taken". A few days later he visited their Pebble Mill studio where he was able to watch the recording. Shortly afterwards he also met the Duke and Duchess of Beaufort where "I related my experiences during some memorable hunts I had with his father 60 years previously."

148

With Geoffrey living so long it was inevitable that other members of the family should die in the intervening years. His younger son Raymond died in 1961, his heart failing him as he was writing a letter in Bulawayo, and the following spring his brother Louis' wife, Olive also died suddenly. The two brothers went on a trip to Scotland to see Dot Arbuthnott, whose husband Jack had died two years earlier. But Louis was taken ill and had to go to hospital for a month before returning home cared for by Mary Weston, whom he later married with Geoffrey acting as his best man.

In 1968 Roger's wife Helen died at Cumnor near Oxford where she was living with Sylvia and Humphry. A memorial service was held for her at Trull church, taken by the vicar Charles Trevelyan, who gave the address, while Louis read the lesson and gave the blessing.

Louis celebrated his 90th birthday with friends and relations, but two years later had a nasty fall and spent his birthday in Torbay Hospital, but, after being operated on, was much improved. Unfortunately the following April he had a bad stroke but "though unable to speak he appeared to understand much of what we said to him." He returned home in May "but he only survived a week, as he passed away peacefully" and was buried with the Bishop of Exeter "giving a very beautiful address." The Newton Abbot police rang peals on the bells before and after the service, as Louis had been in the special police for many years.

Geoffrey continued to do as much as he could, but he had to stop driving after a lorry crashed into his car, as he was reversing. After that he was driven to meets of hounds by friends or went by taxi. He still travelled and loved going hunting or seeing friends and relations, but was based more and more in his flat at Bovey Tracey. In 1978 he reached a notable landmark when he celebrated his 100th birthday with family and friends. On his 102nd birthday the South Devon hounds paraded for him and he was still able to stand briefly and blow his hunting horn. Two months later he passed away.

By this time nothing was left of William Mott's legacy of 1826, but four generations of Motts had been able to live handsomely on the proceeds. William's intention had been to provide for all his children, but principally for his son John. After John's death his estates were to pass to "my grandson William Mott" and then to his sons "in seniority of age and priority of birth". They thus passed briefly to

Charles' eldest brother Willie, and after his death, as he was unmarried, they came unexpectedly, as we have seen, to Roger, Charles' eldest son. All those Motts who benefited directly from William's properties were able to live well and indeed in some style, as Roger and Helen did.

Of the three Motts who feature in this book, Charles and Geoffrey did not benefit in the same way from this inheritance, but they nevertheless lived a lifestyle where they were not lacking in any of the essentials and were able to follow their own enthusiasms. Indeed I am sure that all three Motts would echo the comment that Geoffrey wrote at the end of his memoirs "I have indeed been fortunate in having had so good a time".

All three of them also lived lives where their different characters enabled them to make their mark with a variety of people and in a variety of fields. But for all three their commitment and impact were made essentially in what Charles described as "a quiet sort of way".

APPENDIX A

CHARLES MOTT'S ACCOUNTS

INSURANCE
Life assurance was purchased at the rate of £2-10-0 to £5-0-0 per £100 assured. This was very heavy in relation to an officer's income. Charles Mott's allowances as a captain would be £211-7-11 against premiums of £134.

RENT
When he was at Colchester the cost of renting a house and stable was £13-6-8 per month. In Dawlish they paid £3-13-6 per week; renting a house in Aldershot cost £9-9-0 per month; Portland cost £7-10-0 per month.

MAIN EXPENDITURE
In 1884 Charles calculated all his board and lodging, including household expenses, at £825-4-6. This was made up of:

INSURANCE	COST	OVERALL EXPENDITUE
	£134-0-0	£134-0-0

BOARD AND LODGING		
1st Quarter	£99-2-8	
2nd Quarter	£107-16-4	
3rd Quarter	£105-15-11	
4th Quarter	£93-2-2	£405-17-1

WAGES FOR SERVANTS		
1st Quarter	£12-2-0	
2nd Quarter	£25-16-0	
3rd Quarter	£30-12-0	
4th Quarter	£30-12-0	£99-2-0

DRESS		
1st Quarter	£6-13-3	
2nd Quarter	£3-12-8	
3rd Quarter	£16-5-6	
4th Quarter	£15-6-7	£42-1-0

TRAVEL

In 1884 he calculated his travelling expenses, carriage of baggage, hotels and other incidental expenses at: £70-0-0 (approx)

In 1884 there were also some more significant expenses:

Purchase of horse	£35-18-0	£35-18-0
Purchase of carriage	£27-4-6	£27-4-6
Purchase of pony	£13-3-6	£13-3-6
Horses' keep	£25-10-9	£25-10-9
Miss Slaney	£12-6-8	£12-6-8
Dr McLean	£2-2-0	£2-2-0

TOTAL EXPENDITURE

1882	£904-10-2
1883	£822-17-2
1884	£1035-0-9

EXAMPLES OF EXPENSES

These give a good picture of the way that he lived his life.

For example – May 1882 when the family visited Manadon, St Austell to see the Coodes and Bovey Tracy to see the Holes before moving to Dawlish (see page 40):

1st May	Wife for children 3/6 Post cards 8d
2nd May	Bus 4d Present 1/- Razor 2/- Awl 9d
3rd May	String 6d Stamps 1/- Tobacco 9d
5th May	Bus 3d Wife 2/- Handkerchief and Lanyard 4/- Dinner 4/8 Cigars 10d Theatre 3/- Whisky 8d Punch 3d
7th May	Church collections 1/6
8th May	Washing at Manadon 13/1 Mary's wages for the quarter £5-5-0 Mary's beer money for April 13/- Tumbler 8d Washing 1/7 To Servants at Manadon 10/- Cab 4/- To St Austell and back 19/- Papers 3d
9th May	St Austell to Bodmin and back 3/- Haircut 1/2 Luncheon 2/2
11th May	Crayons 1/-

14th May	Church collections 1/6
15th May	Washing 4/7 To Servants at Trevarthian [Coode's House] 5/- Porters 1/- Tobacco 9d Papers 3d Refreshments 9d To Bovey Tracey 17/6
16th May	Otter Hound 'Cap' 1/-
17th May	To Dawlish and back 3/6 Papers 3d Luncheon 1/8
19th May	Photo 1/9 To Mary £6-1-½ Clarkson 8/- Gayle 1/- Stamps 6d
20th May	Tobacco 8d
22nd May	Servants 8/6 Washing 3/6
23rd May	Porters 1/3 Bovey Tracy to Dawlish 7/- Liquor 15/10 Cake 1/- Paper 1/8 Moving Luggage 3/- Post cards 8d
23rd May	Hire of Bath 3/- Matches 2d Paper 1d Reading Room 3/-
24th May	Net 1/- Stamps 1/- Map 6d Sketch block 5/-
25th May	Subscription to Library 1/9 Teignmouth paper 2d
26th May	Paper and envelope 1½p To Exeter 2/- Paper 2d Cab 1/- Bus 1/- Exeter Cathedral 1/- Cakes 5/2 Cigars 10d Tobacco 1/7 Tram 4d Sausages 9d Refreshments 6d To Dawlish 2/-
27th May	Fowl 2/3 Liquor 7/- Stamps 1/- Gum 1d
28th May	Church collections 2/6
29th May	Brandy 6d
30th May	Boats 5/- To Teignmouth and back 10d Refreshments 10d Evening Papers 6d Crab 1/- Paper 1d Shaving Soap 1/-

DAWLISH WEEKLY BILLS

Lodgings £3-13-6 Oil 1/- Washing linen 9d Etceteras paid by Mrs Friend 3/9 1 lb Butter 1/3 Castors 4d Milk 3/2 Butcher £1-2-8 Grocer £1-8-2 Washing 7/10

31st May	Straw Hat 2/9 Italian band 1/- Cake 1/- 1 Quarter's Insurance Premium £33-10-0 Lena's Quarter's wages £2-2-0 Mary's beer and washing money for the month 13/-

Or January and February 1884 when Charles and Marian were in Ireland with his regiment while the children were looked after in Lichfield (see pages 50-2):

7th January	Sea salt 2/6 Haircut 6d Wife 2/- Frame 6d
	Diary 4/9 Washing 4/1 Boots mended 1/6
	Sarah 5/- Hatchett 1/- Bus 2/- Porter 6d
	Carriage of Box 1/6 Lichfield to Dublin £2-10-0
8th January	Chester 1/6 Stewardess 1/- Porters 1/10
	Breakfast 4/- Papers 5d Cab 2/6 Soap 6d
	Dublin to Listowel £2-12-0 Luncheon 1/4 Porters 1/4
10th January	Stamps 3/- Postal notes 15/2 Envelopes 4/-
11th January	Carriage of Boxes 2/- Washing 1/4
12th January	Newspaper wrappers 7d Cooperative 7/8
	Burrowes' Christmas Box 5/6
13th January	Church collections 1/2
14th January	Wool 1/- Stamps 1/-
15th January	Washing 3/1 Postal order 3/1 Stamps 2/9
16th January	Listowel to Tralee and back 12/2
	Mess bill £1-7-6
17th January	Hotel bill Tralee £1-4-0 Porter 4d Stamps 1/-
	Soap 1/- Mrs Maddox 11/- Pullar's account 8/7
19th January	Stamps 1/- Webb's account £5-18-8
	Dr McLean's account £2-2-0
20th January	Church collections 1/4 Stamps 2/6
21st January	Cheque to Mary at Lichfield £8-0-0
	Wife 5/- To Limerick 16/- Porter 1d
22nd January	Carriage 1/- Suspenders 1/- Sausages 1/1
	Hotel bill 9/3
24th January	Wife 11d Cheese 4/10 Stamps 11d
26th January	Ballybunion 2/6 Church collections 1/4
28th January	Postal orders and stamps 5/2 Wife 3/-
29th January	To Limerick 16/- Carriage 2/- Haircut 6d
	Papers 2d
31st January	Hotel Bill £5-5-10 Wife 1/9 Tobacco 1/8
	Driver 2/- Burrowes' wages 15/-
3rd February	Church collections 2/4
4th February	Stamps 1/6 Washing 2/10 Paint 1/2
6th February	Postal Order 3/- Box mended 2/-

7th February	Stamps 6d Lichfield Bills £8-2-6
8th February	Hotel bill £4-17-10
9th February	Driver 2/- To Tralee and back 9/2
	Biscuits 2½ d Paper 2d Porter 4d
	To Killarney and back 10/-
10th February	Church collection 1/-
11th February	Hotel bill £3-1-6 Servants 4/- Present 3/-
	Porters 1/3 Cab 2/-
15th February	Stamps and parcel post 2/- Eggs 1/6
	Hotel bill £5-2-4 Basket 4d Buttons 2d
	Washing 2/6 Cocoa ¼ Soap 1/-
17th February	Church collections 1/4
18th February	Telegrams 2/- Stamps 2/6
22nd February	Stamps 1/- Dressmaker 2/8 Pullar's account 5/4
	Cobbler 2/- Sketch book 2/6 Telegram 1/-
23rd February	Washing 3/3 Driver 2/-
24th February	Church collections 1/4
25th February	Cheque to Mary £12-12-6 [including her wages]
	Bread and cheese for men 3/6 Washing 2/9
	Irish Times 1/5
26th February	Listowel Hotel Bill £11-19-3 Servants £1-2-0
	Burrowes £1/-/- Hazlewood 7/6 Strap 1/6
	Porters 1/3 To Tralee 7/2 Cloakroom ¼
27th February	Quigley 2/- Cab 4/- Porters 2/5 Telegrams 7/-
	To Killarney 7/6 To Dublin £2-2-0
	Luncheon 1/9 Cabs 5/- Whiskey 1/-
28th February	Shelbourne Hotel Bill £1-12-1 Porters 1/11 Cabs
	12/6 Dogs 2/- To Bangor £1-7-0

Or May 1884 when he was living at Colchester as ADC to General White:

1st May	Annie's wages £1-10-0 Derby lottery £1-0-0
	Stamps 1/- Groom 1/-
2nd May	Copford church 5/- Mrs Naylor 10/-
3rd May	Groom's wages 18/- Chemist 2/6 Stamps 1/-
4th May	Church collection 1/-
6th May	Postal Order 2/2 Stamps 2/- Sweets 4d
	Francis account £3-10-0
	Lay and Wheeler's account £1-12-6

7th May	Postal Orders 2/2 Ablitts account £2-10-0 Groom at Abberton 6d
8th May	Cigar 6d Mrs Naylor 12/6 Stamps 6d
10th May	Washing 7/6 Carriage repaired £2-2-0 Gun 7d Photos 3/- Groom's wages 18/-
11th May	Church collection 1/-
12th May	Morrison's groom 10/- Wife 1/6 General's Groom 1/-
13th May	Ostler 3d Pencil Box 7d
15th May	Hill's account £5-3-0
17th May	Groom's wages 18/- Whiskey 3/6 Mrs Naylor 10/- Washing 2/7 Whiskey 5d Stamps 1/- Coloured Paper 1/7
18th May	Church collections 1/6
20th May	Mary's ticket 2/6 Cab 2/- Bus 8d Powder 8d
21st May	Whiskey 10d Carriage of Parcels ¼ Stamps 1/-
22nd May	Postcards 8d Tobacco 10d
24th May	Household Bills £12-10-0 Papers 7d Groom's wages 18/-
25th May	Church collections 1/3
26th May	To Bury St Edmunds 5/6 Bordshaw 6d Paper 1d
28th May	To London 6/7 Luncheon 1/- Porters 1/- Cab 2/6 Umbrella covered 7/6 Socks and collars 6/6 Academy 2/6 Regimental Dinner £1-1-0 Cigars 4/6
29th May	Breakfast 1/11 Cigar 3d Luncheon 5d Picture 1/- Lord's Cricket Ground 1/- Flower 1/- Whiskey 10d
30th May	Breakfast 1/11 Cigars 6d Luncheon ¼ Cricket at Lord's 8d Cabs 5/6 Porters 9d To Colchester 9/10 Dinner 4/4 Flower 1/- Lodgings 12/- Cab 2/6
31st May	Mrs Naylor 10/- Groom's wages 18/- Household Bills £7-15-0

APPENDIX B

CHARLES MOTT'S PERFORMANCES 1858-1874

DATE	WHERE	PLAY	PART PLAYED	HOW MANY TIMES
December 1857	Dummer House Basingstoke	Box and Cox	Cox	2
December 1858	Dummer House Basingstoke	Domestic Economy Family Pairs	John Grumley Lydia	2
December 1859	Dummer House Basingstoke	My Wife's Mother	Uncle Foozle	2
December 1861	Eton College	Poor Pillicoddy	Mr Pillycoddy	1
9 + 10 September 1865	Moor Hall, Sutton Colefield	'Ariadne' Burlesque Woodcock's Little Game	Bacchus David	2
5 November 1865	Wall, Lichfield	Poor Pillycoddy	Mr Pillycoddy	1
February 1866	Queen's Theatre, Bermuda	Poor Pillycoddy	Mr Pillycoddy	1
April 1866	Queen's Theatre, Bermuda	Send Me Five Shillings 'Aladdin' Burlesque	Mr Golightly Widow Twankey	2
June 1867	School Room Athlone	'Alonzo' Burlesque	Imogene	1
17-18 July 1867	Black's Hotel, Galway	Make Your Wills 'Alonzo' Burlesque	Mrs Foreright Imogene	2
12-13 December 1867	Theatre Royal, Lichfield	Woodcock's Little Game No 1 Round the Corner Thumping Legacy	Mrs Carver Flipper Bambogetti	2
6-7 October 1868	Club House, Aldershot	Who Stole the Pocket Book?	Mr Silvertop	2
17-18 December 1868	Theatre Royal, Lichfield	£100,000 Rosebud of Stinging Nettle Farm Thumping Legacy	General Goodwin Bill Hugley Bambogetti	2
21-22 December 1868	Corn Exchange, Coventry	Plot and Passion 'Patient Penelope' Burlesque Whitebait at Greenwich	Marquis de Cevennes Eurymachus Mr Buzzard	2

9 February 1869	Club House, Aldershot	Swiss Swans The Critic	Burgomaster Dangle	1
30 March 1869	Club House, Aldershot	The Critic	Dangle	1
16 June 1869	Royal Olympic Theatre, London	The Dowager	Sir F. Chasemore	1
28 June 1869	Club House, Aldershot	Little Savage	Major Choker	1
14 July 1869	Gallery of Illustration	Rough Diamond	Sir W Evergreen	1
16-21 August 1869	Theatre Royal, Portsmouth	Flying Scud	Colonel Mulligan	6
23-28 August 1869	Theatre Royal, Southampton	Flying Scud	Colonel Mulligan	6
September 19 1869	Theatre Royal, Ryde, Isle of Wight	£100,000	General Goodwin	1
October 4 1869	Theatre Royal, Ryde, IOW	Unfinished Gentleman	Lord Totterly	1
22 November 1869	Hooton Hall, Cheshire	Bengal Tiger Rosebud of Stinging Nettle Farm	Sir P Pagoda Bill Hugley	1
9 December 1869	Drill Hall, Derby	Bengal Tiger £100,000 Thumping Legacy	Sir P Pagoda General Goodwin Bambogetti	1
16-17 December 1869	Theatre Royal, Lichfield	War to the Knife Bengal Tiger £100,000 Two in the Morning	Mr Harcourt Sir P Pagoda General Goodwin Newpenny	2
23 December 1869	Beacon House, Lichfield	The Dowager	Sir F Chasemore	1
23-24 June 1870	Theatre Royal, Southampton	£100,000 Sisterly Service	General Goodwin Count Delacourt	2
13 July 1870	Theatre Royal, Portsmouth	£100,000	General Goodwin	1
21-23 July 1870	Old Theatre Royal, Bristol	Happy Pair	Mr Honeyton	3
25-29 July 1870	Theatre Royal, Bath	Happy Pair	Mr Honeyton	5
17 August 1870	Theatre Royal, Portsmouth	Progress	John Ferne	1
22-27 August 1870	Theatre Royal, Brighton	Progress	John Ferne	6

Date	Venue	Play	Role	No.
29 August – 3 Sept 1870	Theatre Royal, Brighton	Mrs Deadset	Captain	6
19 September 1870	Theatre Royal, Ryde IOW	Frederick of Prussia	Frederick	1
26 September 1870	Theatre Royal, Ryde IOW	Delicate Ground	Alphonse	1
7 October 1870	Theatre Royal, Ryde IOW	Our Wife	Marquis de Ligny	1
20-21 October 1870	Town Hall, Ryde, IOW	David Garrick Scenes from Richard III, Othello and Romeo and Juliet Checkmate	Simon Ingot Clarence Iago Romeo Sir E Toffee	2
February 1871	Beaconfield, Plymouth	Area belle	Tosser	1
31 March 1871	Theatre Royal, Exeter	£100,000	General Goodwin	1
15-18 November 1781	Royal Music Hall, Leamington	Wanted a Wife Rough Diamond 'William Tell' Burlesque Sisterly Service Turn him out	Sir W Armitage Sir W Evergreen Emma Count Delacour Nicodemus Nobbs	4
13 February 1872	Fort Tregantle, Cornwall	No one round the Corner	Flipper	1
12 March 1872	Fort Tregantle, Cornwall	Two in the Morning	Newpenny	1
8 August 1872	Theatre Royal, Exeter	£100,000	General Goodwin	1
14 August 1872	Theatre Royal, Plymouth	£100,000 Whitebait at Greenwich	General Goodwin Glimmer	1
21 August 1872	Theatre Royal, Plymouth	The Steeplechase	Dr Clipper	1
19-20 September 1872	Bijou Theatre, Paignton	£100,000 Ticket of Leave Man	General Goodwin Melter Moss	2
14 November 1872	Theatre Royal, Portsmouth	Happy Pair	Mr Honeyton	1
15 April 1873	Theatre Royal, Exeter	Not a Bad Judge Delicate Ground	Marquis de Trevre Citizen Sangfroid	
19 April 1873	Theatre Royal, Bath	Not a Bad Judge	Marquis de Trevre	1

		Cool as a Cucumber Rosebud of Stinging Nettle Farm Behind Lime Thumping Legacy Chimney Corner Warlock of the Glen To Paris and Back for £5	Plumber Squire Chiryn Jeremiah Fluke Jerry Ominous Peter Probity Samuel Snizzle	
January, February, March 1874	Barracks, *Castleton* Co Mayo			8
December 1874	Manadon, Plymouth	Done on Both Sides	Pygmalion Phibbs	1

TOTAL NUMBER OF PERFORMANCES	103

160

APPENDIX C

FAMILY TREES

Mott Family Tree
Parlby Family Tree
Kynaston Family Tree
Hill Family Tree
Oakeley Family Tree

MOTT FAMILY TREE

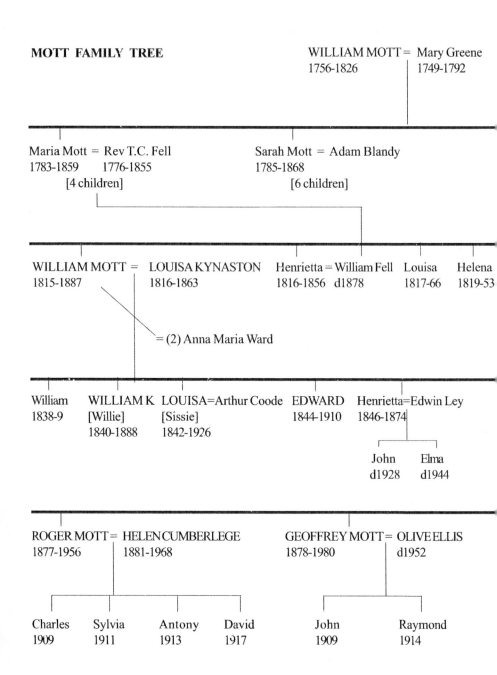

WILLIAM MOTT = Mary Greene
1756-1826   1749-1792

Maria Mott = Rev T.C. Fell   Sarah Mott = Adam Blandy
1783-1859   1776-1855   1785-1868
      [4 children]   [6 children]

WILLIAM MOTT = LOUISA KYNASTON   Henrietta = William Fell   Louisa   Helena
1815-1887   1816-1863   1816-1856 d1878   1817-66   1819-53

= (2) Anna Maria Ward

William   WILLIAM K   LOUISA=Arthur Coode   EDWARD   Henrietta=Edwin Ley
1838-9   [Willie]   [Sissie]   1844-1910   1846-1874
           1840-1888   1842-1926

                                                        John   Elma
                                                        d1928   d1944

ROGER MOTT = HELEN CUMBERLEGE   GEOFFREY MOTT = OLIVE ELLIS
1877-1956   1881-1968   1878-1980   d1952

Charles   Sylvia   Antony   David   John   Raymond
1909   1911   1913   1917   1909   1914

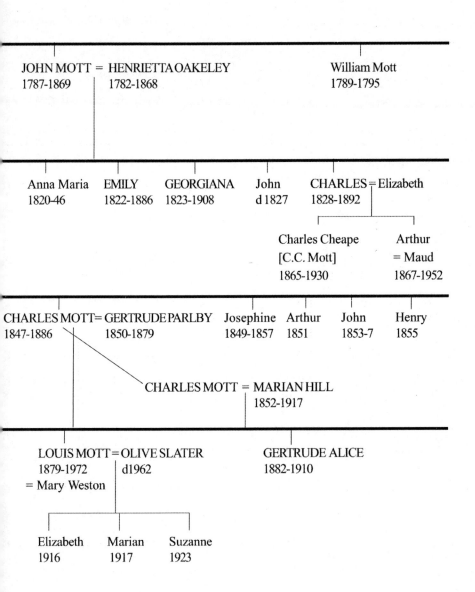

JOHN MOTT = HENRIETTA OAKELEY   William Mott
1787-1869   1782-1868   1789-1795

Anna Maria   EMILY   GEORGIANA   John   CHARLES = Elizabeth
1820-46   1822-1886   1823-1908   d 1827   1828-1892

                                                  Charles Cheape   Arthur
                                                  [C.C. Mott]   = Maud
                                                  1865-1930   1867-1952

CHARLES MOTT= GERTRUDE PARLBY   Josephine   Arthur   John   Henry
1847-1886   1850-1879   1849-1857   1851   1853-7   1855

                          CHARLES MOTT = MARIAN HILL
                                         1852-1917

LOUIS MOTT = OLIVE SLATER   GERTRUDE ALICE
1879-1972   d1962   1882-1910
= Mary Weston

Elizabeth   Marian   Suzanne
1916   1917   1923

163

PARLBY FAMILY TREE

John Alexander Parlby = Letitia Hall
1769-1849 | 1772-1848
[HEIRESS OF MANADON]

REVEREND JOHN HALL PARLBY = [1] Emily Holder
1805-1899 |
[OF MANADON] |

BLANCHE PARLBY
1840-1881

GERALD PARLBY = Adela Kerrison
1842-1894 ['Winkie']

REVEREND JOHN HALL PARLBY = [2] EMMA RADCLIFFE
1805-1899 | 1821-1894
[OF MANADON]

Florence	GERTRUDE = CHARLES MOTT	MILDRED	MARION = Charles	ST JOHN
1846-1871	1850-1879 1847-1886	1852-1895	1854-1930 Arbuthnott	1855-188
		[MILLIE]		

ROGER	GEOFFREY	LOUIS	John [Jack] = Dorothy [Dot
1877	1878	1879	Viscount
			Arbuthnott

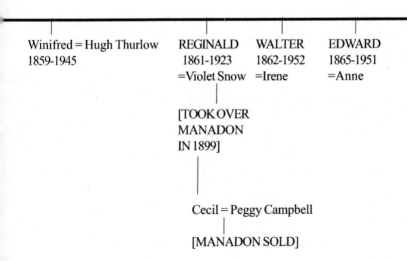

EMILY PARLBY = WILLIAM HOLE
1841-1926   [OF PARKE, BOVEY TRACEY]

Winifred = Hugh Thurlow   REGINALD   WALTER   EDWARD
1859-1945   1861-1923   1862-1952   1865-1951
                            =Violet Snow =Irene   =Anne

                            [TOOK OVER
                            MANADON
                            IN 1899]

                            Cecil = Peggy Campbell

                            [MANADON SOLD]

KYNASTON FAMILY TREE

Thomas Kynaston = Ann Jone
1734-1804

ANNE KYNASTON = THOMAS BRETT
1767   of SPRING GROVE, KENT
1758-1832
[Children died without issue]

Letitia Kynaston = William Selwyn
1774-1842

George Selwyn
Bishop of Lichfield 1867

John Selwyn
Bishop of Melanesia
[Second cousin of Charles Mott]

ROGER KYNASTON = Juliana Browne
1805-1874
[No issue]

[Inherited Spring Grove, Kent which he left
to his nephew William Kynaston Mott
who left it to his nephew Roger Mott]

HERBERT KYNASTON = Elizabeth Kenned
1809-1878
[No issue]

[He was High Master of St Paul's School]

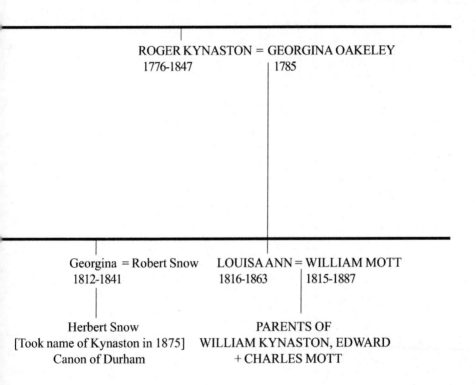

ROGER KYNASTON = GEORGINA OAKELEY
1776-1847   1785

Georgina = Robert Snow   LOUISA ANN = WILLIAM MOTT
1812-1841   1816-1863   1815-1887

Herbert Snow   PARENTS OF
[Took name of Kynaston in 1875]   WILLIAM KYNASTON, EDWARD
Canon of Durham   + CHARLES MOTT

HILL FAMILY TREE

REVEREND RICHARD HILL = SARAH THOMAS
1824-1891

CHARLES MOTT = [2] MARIAN — ALICE — LOUISE — JOHN — RICHARD = EMILY — QUINTIN = ELIZABETH — HUMPHRY = EDITH — MAUDE = JOHN
1847-1886   1852-1917   1853   1855   1856   1858-1939   ELLIS   1859   BARTON   1862   TAYLOR   1865   KNIGHT

GERTRUDE ALICE MOTT
1882-1910

= [1] GERTRUDE PARLBY
1850-1879

ROGER MOTT = HELEN CUMBERLEGE
1877-1956   1881-1968

SYLVIA MOTT ════ 1936 ════ HUMPHRY
1911   1903

OAKELEY FAMILY TREE

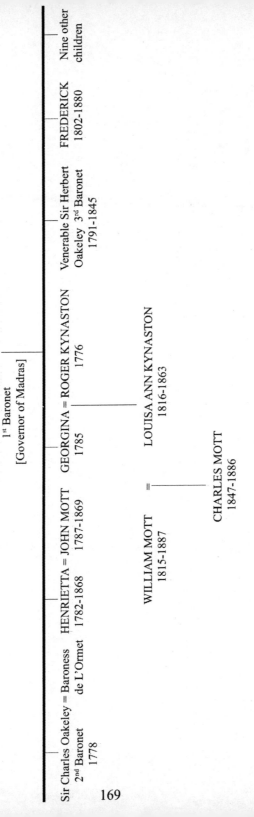

SIR CHARLES OAKELEY = Helena Beatson
1st Baronet
[Governor of Madras]

Sir Charles Oakeley = Baroness de L'Ormet
2nd Baronet
1778

HENRIETTA = JOHN MOTT
1782-1868   1787-1869

GEORGINA = ROGER KYNASTON
1785   1776

Venerable Sir Herbert Oakeley 3rd Baronet
1791-1845

FREDERICK
1802-1880

Nine other children

WILLIAM MOTT
1815-1887

=

LOUISA ANN KYNASTON
1816-1863

CHARLES MOTT
1847-1886